Lowell Thomas

The Stranger Everyone Knows

Lowell Thomas
The Stranger Everyone Knows

America's most illustrious newsman as colleagues and others have seen him through the last five decades.

Profiles by Russel Crouse, Francis Yeats-Brown, H. Allen Smith, Maurice Zolotov, Eleanor Harris, Dale Carnegie and others.

With illustrations from his personal collection.

Edited by Norman R. Bowen

DOUBLEDAY & COMPANY, INC.
Garden City, N. Y.

Preface

To Lowell Thomas, 1967 was just another exhilarating news year of history in the making.

He broadcasts every week-day as usual (the longest daily program in radio history—now in its 39th year.)

He speaks and talks his way around the world, never able to balance requests with his available time.

He is working on a couple of books and reluctantly facing up to writing his memoirs. (Since 1924, he has authored 51 books, including many best sellers.)

He is planning another expedition or two, although it becomes more difficult each year to find remote or "forbidden" areas that he doesn't know as well as his own backyard.

He remains an avid sportsman and skiier, traveling weekly to his favorite far-flung snow or golf courses, renewing fond associations with the great and not-so-great.

But 1967 was a special year that brought with it two reasons for this book's being:

1. Lowell Thomas on April 6, 1967 noted (actually, ignored) his 75th birthday.

2. On August 4, 1967, Lowell and Fran Thomas observed their Golden Wedding Anniversary. (And even Lowell knew that was one date not to be ignored.)

And there are some fine people in Ohio (the state of Lowell's birth and home of his ancestors) and Colorado (where he grew to young manhood and embarked on his phenomenal career) who have established museums in his honor to keep for posterity the living history Lowell Thomas has seen and reported.

This book is published for those who visit the two museums and also for Lowell's global audience—the millions who instantly recognize the best-known voice in the world but have not yet had an opportunity to meet the man himself. And a rare man he is.

Lowell is much too busy to take a look back, even at his own unparalleled career. He looks ahead. And, despite their three-quarter-century use, his mild blue eyes are as steady and observant and keen as ever. Amazingly, his step, his pace, his verve, his ambitious schedule match those of men 20 years his junior.

So in this book, we're taking a brief look back for Lowell at the beginnings of his legendary career which catapulted him to the top of the journalistic world, and at the more than a half-century since, during which time he has *stayed* at the top.

No other journalist or world figure, with the possible exception of Winston Churchill, has remained in the public spotlight as long. In every decade articles have appeared in the press of the world about Lowell Thomas.

Thus, to tell his story, we have selected a dozen or so representative articles, from as many different sources, ranging in origin from Alaska to India. They have only one thing in common—the subject.

It is interesting to see how each astute analyst views this subject—how each trained professional observer sees the man.

It also is of interest to note the different style of each writer, many of them famous bylines in their own right.

Most significant are the revolutionary changes made in journalistic techniques during the five decades of Lowell's career. In no half-century has man's communicative ability advanced so fast. Lowell's working press days span the epochal era from the legendary Chicago newspaper days of Ben Hecht and Charles MacArthur of the Twenties through the development of newer media—films, newsreels, radio and television—of the Thirties, Forties, Fifties and Sixties. With a few refinements like Cinerama thrown in.

The discerning reader is sure to discover that the various writers don't always agree on certain details. The obvious explanation is this: when journalists do pieces for magazines they nearly always do their writing in a hurry and without double-checking as to accuracy—the sort of accuracy you would expect in a more carefully written biography. Actually, profiles are more valuable for the impression they give rather than for such things as dates, etc.

We think you'll enjoy reading of Lowell's adventures and exploits over the years as related by different writers. A subtitle for this volume could read "Lowell Thomas Down the Decades."

Anyway, he still remains the world's best traveling companion.

Included, wherever possible, are personal glimpses of Lowell Thomas The Man, in order to help explain it all. The profiles that follow for the most part are written by journalists and authors who knew him well.

We are indebted to Lowell's long-time secretarial right-hand, Electra, for invaluable assistance digging through Lowell's scrapbooks and files. And to Richford Scopes, an Alta (Utah) ski enthusiast like Lowell, for art design and layout, and to O. Preston Robinson for over-all supervision.

Finally, we wish to express appreciation to the following publications:

Reader's Digest, The Landmark of London, Argosy, Coronet, This Week, Newsweek, Ski, Sports Illustrated, Pathfinder and Bombay Mirror; to the N. Y. Herald Tribune, The Cincinnati Times-Star, The Juneau Empire (Alaska) and the Yukon Daily News, and to the individual authors for permission to reprint their work.

—Norman R. Bowen

To Frances Ryan Thomas, the lovely lady who for half a century has put up so patiently with a peripatetic pilgrim as he proceeded along his "Golden Road To Samarkand."

Contents

Introduction

Editor Norman Bowen has asked me for some comments on what he hath wrought. Here they are:—

Why all these profiles? I suspect he is putting them in to fill up the spaces between the pictures. Why all the pictures? I suspect they are to fill up the spaces between the profiles.

This anthology—or whatever you would call it—of pieces written about me, isn't a good idea at all; and I hope you won't believe what you read if you go beyond this page. However if you do, I suggest you limit your reading to the excerpt from "To Hell In A Handbasket," which has nothing biographical about it. I have long hoped to cross H. Allen Smith's trail again. I wanted to tell him about an aftermath-incident that followed our Prohibition Era "literary" wing-ding.

When the last celebrity (?) staggered into our Sutton Place elevator or slid down the stairs, I went to my bedroom on the floor above, to calm down, and think over this unexpected catastrophe into which we had stumbled. There sprawled across my bed was as beautiful a blonde as you'd ever hope to see—out cold.

Hurriedly I dashed downstairs again, to see if by chance my wife might have gone out to a nearby delicatessen or somewhere. She hadn't. So, I returned to the bedroom, gingerly tapped the young lady—on her cheek. Whereupon she opened her eyes, and with a startled look, but not a sound, jumped from the bed, dashed for the elevator, and vanished. I had hoped maybe H. Allen Smith, or our mutual friend editor Jimmy Monahan, might have known who she was.

Fran's mother had recently arrived from Denver. After meeting some of the critics and others who took part in the affair described by H. Allen Smith, and having a look at the many holes burned in the carpets and rugs belonging to Mr. and Mrs. Owen D. Young, from whom we had subleased the duplex, she asked her daughter to explain just what kind of friends we had! So, you might be interested in H. Allen Smith's account of what happened that day, and how it came about.

Why aren't the other authors to be trusted? For the simple reason that nearly all of them are, or were, my close friends, so naturally they wouldn't cut me to pieces.

The first article or profile, or whatever it is, was turned out almost half a century ago by one of Britain's top airmen in World War One. Captain Alan Bott was the author of the first book ever written about air warfare. Entitled "Cavalry of the Clouds" it was the story of his own experiences as a fighter pilot on the Western Front. Those were the days before we had entered the war, and along with Ian Hay, and other British heroes who were glamorous and exceptionally articulate, this young airman was sent over to help nudge us into the war. Alan Bott and I became pals, a friendship that increased with a bit of low key British intensity when after the war I turned up in London telling the story of Lawrence and Allenby. The shock of an American troubadour putting on a show in praise of the valor of the British, without a word of any sort about what Americans had done in the war, that shock literally overwhelmed many of our cousins across the Atlantic. Hence this piece about me written for a British publication by my English flying friend.

As for Major Francis Yeats-Brown, the Bengal Lancer, I believe "Y.B." would have taken off on a rocket for Mars if I had asked him to do so. Yeats-Brown was a poet and a scholar. It was just an accident of birth that sent "Y.B." to Sandhurst, then on as a subaltern in the Indian army, and next as an aviator shot down in Mesopotamia. "Out East" he was imprisoned and then made his escape from the dread Turkish prison of Afion Kara Hisar. After the war he was in command of the 18th Bengal Lancers at Cawnpore. All this was because as the fourth son of a distinguished English diplomat there was no place for him to go but into the army —first son to succeed the father; second son the Royal Navy; third son the Church; the fourth the Army. To his dying day "Y.B." was grateful to me because I "borrowed" him from Lord Rawlinson's army, and took him on a long expedition that in eighteen months covered far more of the subcontinent of Hindustan than he had seen in eighteen years as a dashing officer representing the British Raj.

Yeats-Brown had so much fun on his jaunt with me he resigned from the army, became the editor of the famous London Spectator, wrote his best seller autobiography "The Lives of a Bengal Lancer," and went on to further literary triumphs.

For a variety of reasons, I'm sure no one could have paid my long time companion the Bengal Lancer enough rupees to cause him to say anything unkind about the fellow who had pried him loose from a career for which he always insisted he was not cut out. He was a gallant and brave officer in the Indian army, as well as in the RAF. His fellow officers vouched for this. But, they also agreed that "Y.B." was not in the Kipling tradition, and they considered him "half mad" because he often donned native costumes.

Another of these pieces is by that character of world wide renown, Dale Carnegie of "How To Win Friends And Influence People" fame. Dale was "on my side" because I also had pried him loose from the rather prosaic career on which he at first was launched. Although I had my own selfish reasons for luring him away, that could not have influenced dynamic Dale to the point where he could have said anything critical of me.

It was like this: Dale Carnegie—(Carnagey he then spelled it) —had recently come from a Missouri farm. He was all hepped up on the subject of effective speaking. I stumbled on him by chance, in New York at Carnegie Hall, where he soon decided to change the spelling of his own name so it would be the same as the steel tycoon who had launched libraries all over America. After all Dale was a born showman, of a rather special Missouri type. I had asked him to criticize a speech I was to deliver in Washington. Like my father, all my life I've been "going to school," hunting for experts to show me how to do things better. That was how I found Dale Carnegie. Later when I had an unexpected success on the platform in London, I got the Napoleonic complex, decided to conquer the world with second and third string companies, and brought Dale across the Atlantic to organize these, train the speakers, and then manage the whole operation—while Fran and I went off to Australia to have fun.

Long before I got back Dale had put the project into near bankruptcy, and himself in the hospital with a nervous breakdown. From that day on I don't believe Dale Carnegie ever looked back. From that day on, working, promoting his original effective speaking formula, he did nothing but make money on a bigger and bigger scale, until he finally became almost as rich as Croesus.

There are few things more salutary than losing your shirt and everybody elses, when you are still young. That gives you plenty of time for a comeback, and the way Dale Carnegie came back from that debacle when he was managing things for me in the British Isles, is an epic story. Dale in his way was a genius.

After he had written his famous book "How To Win Friends and Influence People," which sold all over the world almost as widely as the Bible, and for which I wrote an introduction, Dale turned out another tome entitled "How To Stop Worrying and Start Living." In this he saluted me in the following manner: "This book is dedicated to a man who doesn't need to read it—Lowell Thomas."

From this you can judge what type profile my friend Dale Carnegie would be likely to write. So why bother reading it?

Almost all of these pieces were written by people who were either closely associated with me, or who were—I hope still are—my friends. So you may have a little difficulty finding anything here to offset the generous remarks made by them.

Couldn't the editor of this book, Utah Journalist Norm Bowen, have found some caustic pieces to include, to spice it up? Haven't I ever been attacked in print? Am I not vulnerable? I am indeed! Were all the critical pieces thrown in the waste basket long ago? Maybe so. Or were they limited to brief, caustic paragraphs. I can remember one that shook me up. After our Allenby-Lawrence season at the Royal Opera House and at Royal Albert Hall in London, the then Prime Minister of Australia, the legendary Billy Hughes, invited Fran and me to do a tour of Australia, and New Zealand. This was long before you could jet to the Antipodes in a matter of hours. In 1919 it took us six weeks to make the voyage by sea; and it was while we were there, almost cut off from the rest of the globe, that Dale Carnegie ran our ship aground on unexpected shoals in the British Isles.

The Australian and New Zealand cavalry, and their airmen too, had played a major role in driving the Turks from the Holy Land. That was why the Prime Minister had extended his invitation. He and his cabinet gave a banquet for us at Government House, and then we launched our tour before a joint session of the Australian Parliament.

There was a new weekly magazine in Sydney, whose editors

were smart enough to know that one of the sure ways to get readers is to attack nearly everybody. It's a formula that works. Although other publications in Australia were cordial and generous, *The Sydney Bulletin* gave me quite a lambasting. The sentence I'll never forget, the one that cut deepest, went about as follows: "After seeing the Lowell Thomas show we concluded the Palestine campaign had been won by Allenby, Lawrence and an American named Lowell Thomas."

Actually attacks of that kind, even if they leave scars, may be good for you. I'm sure *The Sydney Bulletin* article put me on my mettle, and caused me to do a better job on my Down Under tour than I might otherwise have done.

I know of at least one profile that might have been included in this book—*if* it had been written.

If you were a Westerner and had spent your boyhood there in the days when it was still rugged frontier country, you would consider yourself a member of a special esoteric group. Having spent my youth in a roaring gold mining camp high in the Colorado Rockies, this meant I had something special in common with such friends in later life as Tex Rickard, Jack Dempsey, Elsa Maxwell, Texas Guinan, Eddie Eagan, Damon Runyon, Gene Fowler, and many others—including one Harold Ross, founder and editor of the *New York Magazine*. I was from the Cripple Creek District while Harold was from the once booming silver camp of Aspen, on the other slope of the Rockies, not many miles down the road from Leadville.

When Harold Ross launched the *New Yorker* he had the usual problem of building circulation, and he used the same formula I had run into in Sydney, Australia. Many of the early *New Yorker* profiles were written in vitriol.

My fellow Coloradoan, when I would meet him at The Dutch Treat Club, would say, "Lowell, I'm going to send one of our writers up to do a profile on you." With a sickly smile I would say: "Send him along, Harold."

Finally a *New Yorker* writer arrived on Quaker Hill. When he phoned me in advance I began to think of how I might upset his plans. First I urged him to bring his wife, and plan to stay as long as possible, as our guests. That was in the days when I had my somewhat notorious ball team, "The Nine Old Men," the team that for years played an annual game with our Dutchess County neighbor President Roosevelt, who called his team the "Roosevelt Packers" the year he was attempting to pack The Supreme Court.

When the Harold Ross writer arrived he turned out to be a brilliant young Irish-American. You would know his name if I mentioned it, for he is still going strong, a top critic. I assumed his assignment would be to "do a job" on me, one that might bring in more subscribers, and all that.

One of the first things I asked was whether he had ever played ball. When he said yes, with enthusiasm, I invited him to play second base on a team that included humorist Lew Lehr, speed flyer Frank Hawks, cartoonist Paul Webb (the hillbillies), Munro Leaf (Ferdinand the Bull), Gene Sarazen, Gene Tunney, and others.

Later when he returned to New York, so far as I knew nothing was ever written. But, two or three years later as he passed me on Fifth Avenue one day he called out: "They are all set to run that profile next week!" and then laughed.

Anyhow what a fine guy he was to let me get away with it.

One of the profiles published here includes a remark made many years ago by a foreign correspondent for whom I had great admiration. He name was Walter Duranty. There have been few to equal Walter, whom I had first known shortly after he left his assignment as a Cambridge Don, went off to World War One, lost a leg, and then joined Wythe Williams in the Paris office of the *New York Times*. Duranty said I had pulled off the number one journalistic scoop of the era with my "discovery" of Lawrence of Arabia.

In a way I suppose this was true. But for half a century now I've been kicking myself around the block for not covering the Arabian campaign more completely and for not doing a far better job with the story that I brought back about Lawrence. I had the chance of a lifetime, and nearly everyone thinks I made the most of it. Actually, I didn't. For one thing I hurried away from Arabia much too soon. I was too eager to get back to the Western Front and see what our American doughboys were doing in the Argonne. However, to some small degree I recently have tried to make up for this by bringing out a new edition of my "With Lawrence in Arabia," to which I have added a new prologue and an epilogue.

In the former I have tried to make amends to T. E. Lawrence

by defending him against the vicious attacks made by writers who have belittled him. In the epilogue I tell about some almost equally remarkable Britishers who were associated with Lawrence in the Arabian campaign.

As for the pictures rounded up by my Utah friend Norman Bowen, my long time manager and business colleague, Frank M. Smith, to whom I also am overwhelmingly indebted for getting me out of many a tight financial spot and for at least temporarily making me solvent, he's to blame for the pictures. Frank Smith was the genius who made our Cinerama organization a huge financial success. Later he created a television and radio empire now well known as Capital Cities Broadcasting.

On one of his frequent visits to my Quaker Hill broadcasting and film studio, he saw a few pictures of me, in company with famous people. This gave him an idea, and he asked Electra, for more than thirty years my Girl Friday, if in her spare time she would go through the files and scrapbooks, and see how many more such pictures she could find. His idea was to put them on the wall of one of the Capital Cities offices in New York. Electra soon came up with several hundred such pictures, and has been finding more and more of them ever since. Where did they all come from, why so many? Here's the story:

More than half a century ago when I made my first two journeys to the Klondike, down the Yukon, and to various parts of Alaska, I carried my own cameras, the heavy equipment of that day. The conclusion I came to was, if you are going on expeditions, if you are interested in making film productions of any kind, the smart thing is to hire the most capable cameraman you can find. For half a century this has been my strategy. All of my journeys have been for the dual purpose of gathering material for books and articles, and for motion pictures. So, every time we have encountered interesting people, "stills" also have been made of them. In addition to this, acting as master of ceremonies at so many functions down through the years has involved me in events where commercial photographers have always been banging away.

The pictures editor Bowen is using are only a few of what Electra found in going through our files, an assignment which she says she'll never be able to finish.

One thing more: There ought to be at least a few pages in this book telling about my failures and my wasted opportunities, my endless mistakes, and above all about the hard time I have given my inspiring, patient and long-suffering wife who has gone with me nearly everywhere and has done so much to help me and spur me on during these past five decades. Never during the many years when the going was rough, never did she express the slightest doubt about what I did. Oh she criticized my work, corrected mistakes I made on the platform, but her supreme confidence made all the difference. So I'm just another fellow lucky enough to have married the right girl. And what could be more important than that?

Solong,

Presidential Tributes

THE WHITE HOUSE

WASHINGTON

November 12, 1965

Dear Walter:

Long before jet airliners had shrunk the world,
Lowell Thomas had it in his pocket. He is one
of those persons who has been everywhere --
twice.

It seems to me that curiosity and alertness are
the twin keys to his great career. Lowell Thomas
has always wanted to know what was going on in
the world. In finding out, he took us on some de-
lightful trips to strange places.

I am happy to join your group tonight in honoring
a man whose influence on tens of millions of
listeners and readers cannot be measured.

Sincerely,

Mr. Walter Cronkite
Columbia Broadcasting System
524 West 57th Street
New York, N. Y. 10019

It is not too often that the President of the United States participates in a testimonial banquet. When *three* Presidents do so, the man being honored can only be Lowell Thomas.

America's most enduring public figure and newsman was acclaimed by 1200 friends meeting at the Waldorf Astoria Hotel in New York, Nov. 22, 1965. Sponsored by the broadcasting industry in cooperation with The Dutch Treat Club, The Marco Polo Club and The Explorers Club, the affair was "an expression of appreciation for the many fine contributions he has made to the field of communications, for his warm and deep concern for his fellow man, and for his devotion to the Nation."

Interspersed with entertainment and friendly spoofs were many tributes, including the rare messages from ex-Presidents Truman and Eisenhower and President Johnson reproduced here. Among the many notable speakers were Governor Nelson Rockefeller of New York and former Governor Thomas E. Dewey. General chairman was newsman Walter Cronkite, with Arthur Godfrey in charge of entertainment.

TAPED MESSAGE TO L. T. FROM GENERAL EISENHOWER

SALUTE TO LOWELL THOMAS NIGHT - NOV. 22, 1965

Hello Lowell --

This is "Ike" Eisenhower, with you this evening thanks to the electronic wonder of the tape recorder -- wishing you many more years of successful speaking and writing and exploring. Of course, on the last point you have seen just about everything in the world that is worth seeing. Indeed it might be very difficult for you to find a spot on the earth that you have not thoroughly examined. Your zest for new places and your vigor in reaching them suggests one possibility - your enrollment as an astronaut. Should you need a recommendation don't fail to call on me, worthless though it may be. While I could not provide you with the certainty of a round trip, I could at least wish you good luck.

HARRY S TRUMAN
INDEPENDENCE, MISSOURI
November 22, 1965

Dear Walter:

I am genuinely sorry that I can't be with you tonight to pay my respects and esteem to the Methuselah of radio broadcasts. He deserves all he will get from his emulators tonight!

I only have the kindest feeling for him - but then I was never much for seeking approval or adulation from you gentlemen of the press - and, I might add that, while he never helped me much, he rarely, if ever, hurt me.

Lowell, have a wonderful evening! Keep up the good work - for years and years to come!

Sincerely yours,

Harry Truman

Mr. Walter Cronkhite, Chairman
Salute to Lowell Thomas Dinner
c/o The Explorers Club
46 East 70th Street
New York, New York 10021

SECTION 1

As the result of such phenomenally successful theater productions as "Life With Father," and the more recent "Sound of Music," Russel Crouse long was the favorite of millions.

What some may have overlooked was the fact that he was one of America's most talented writers of articles, books, anything to attract his boundless enthusiasm.

Just read the following profile by Mr. Crouse,—it appeared in the Reader's Digest in 1961—and see if you don't agree.

Yes, There Is a Lowell Thomas

By RUSSEL CROUSE *Co-author of the Broadway hits, "Life With Father," "The Sound of Music," etc.*

There are several theories about Lowell Thomas, one of which is that he is not a man but a legend that has been running around the world in a blue-serge suit for longer than most men can remember. This postulate is based on the reasonable contention that no mortal could possibly do all the things credited to this globe-trotting, history-chasing, book-writing, broadcasting, movie-making phenomenon known as Lowell Thomas.

Do you believe there's a flesh-and-blood man whose trips around the world are almost as frequent as yours to the corner drugstore; who uses airplanes the way you and I use the family car; who has a whole mountain range (in Antarctica) named after him; who started taking snap-shots with a Brownie and wound up with Cinerama; who has dined with practicing cannibals without becoming part of the dinner; who has more degrees than a thermometer; who has more "firsts" to his credit than any other man, with the possible exception of Adam?

Well, it is my duty to assure you that there *is* a real Lowell Thomas. First, let's dispose of the legend that he was born in the middle of the Sahara Desert on skis, that he surprised the attending obstetrician with the greeting "Good evening, everybody," and that he then took off over a mountain and has been climbing, sliding, flying—and *talking*—ever since, until now mountains run screaming when he approaches, deserts rise up and throw sand in his face, and microphones get "Thomas-fright" when he enters a broadcasting studio.

Now let's replace all this with the facts. They prove that Lowell Thomas the man is even more fabulous than the fable.

The evidence begins with an entry in the archives of Darke County, Ohio, recording the birth of Lowell Jackson Thomas on April 6, 1892. His parents were both schoolteachers. His father, Harry George Thomas, was a student of everything under and beyond the sun (in 1952 he was still taking college courses, at the age of 82). Soon after Lowell was born, Harry Thomas was graduated from medical school, and decided to set up practice at the end of his own particular rainbow, where others, literally, had found their pot of gold.

This was the incredible Eldorado on the slope of Pikes Peak in Colorado known as the Cripple Creek gold camp, which in its heyday yielded half a billion dollars in the yellow metal. Half a million fortune hunters trooped in and out of Cripple Creek. They spent their days below the ground digging wealth—or stealing it. Many of the veins were so rich that no one missed the gold a "highgrader" took out in his pockets, his trouser cuffs, his lunch box or his mouth. Their nights were spent in saloons—there were as many as ten to a block—gambling halls, dance dives and a district where the red lights were not traffic signals.

Young Lowell Thomas grew up in this atmosphere. He sold papers in and out of the saloons and gambling halls. He learned to carry a gun, much as you would an umbrella, because every man needed one in a region where it rained bullets frequently. He played baseball on the side of a peak where if you slid into third base you might keep on going down the mountain a mile or so. To get to Sunday school he had to walk through the red-light district, and he did, clutching tightly the hand of his Sunday-school teacher, a girl named Texas Guinan (later famous as queen of New York's "Speakeasy Era").

All this boisterous activity, of course, took place on the wrong side of the railroad tracks. But culturally the Thomas home was on the right side. When a miner had an extra dollar he bought a drink; when Dr. Harry Thomas had an extra dollar he bought a book. Within a die's throw from the dice tables he assembled a fine library that covered philosophy, mathematics, geology, comparative religion, astronomy and medicine. Young Lowell absorbed it all.

Doctor Thomas had the quaint notion that life could be much simpler for the person who had been taught to speak clearly and distinctly, and he began to work on Lowell at the age of five. By the time the boy was ten, he knew the recitable works of virtually all the major and minor poets and was ready to declaim them at the drop of a hat.

He perorated at Fourth of July picnics, and he followed the

3

apple pie at every Sunday-school potluck supper. He charged with the Light Brigade, he praised Caesar and he kept the bridge with Horatius.

Occasionally, meeting his son on the street, Doctor Thomas would lead the way to a church where he would stand Lowell in the pulpit, take a seat in the last pew and instruct the young man to discourse on the Vale of Kashmir or some other place they had been reading about.

"Aspirate your h's!" he would shout at the young orator. And Lowell would aspirate until idlers in the pool hall down the street complained that they could no longer concentrate on their idling.

The first opportunity young Lowell had to make use of his eloquence came unexpectedly when Doctor Thomas, sensing the end of Cripple Creek's boom, decided to look around the West for a new opportunity. While he looked, his wife and son returned to Ohio for a year. Lowell, 15, enrolled in Greenville High School.

It began as a miserable year. The school heroes were the football players. Lowell didn't make the team. Then, one day, an anti-athletic English teacher decreed that all the boys in the class should learn a famous oration and recite it before the school assembly. To most of the students that was a scholastic death warrant.

On the fateful day a parade of tongue-tied, faltering Ciceros crossed the platform. Then lightning struck. With complete assurance, young Thomas launched into Wendell Phillips' fiery tribute to Toussaint L'Ouverture, the hero of Haiti. It was no contest. Lowell's victory was inevitable. But the reward was astonishing. He was elected captain of the football team!

The incident not only proved Doctor Thomas's contention that eloquence was a virtue, it made Lowell realize that he was going to continue to talk and therefore he needed something to talk about. He decided to get as much education as he could, as rapidly as possible. To this end, and earning his way, he enrolled in both the freshman and sophomore classes at the University of Northern Indiana (now Valparaiso University). He graduated in two years with two degrees, B.S. and M.A., and went back to Cripple Creek riding an academic cloud. But when he applied for a job at the mines, they handed him a pick and shovel.

Now it's difficult to shovel while holding a master's degree in one hand. So Lowell decided that if he couldn't talk for a living, the next best thing was to write. He began as a reporter on the Cripple Creek *Times* and within a few months was the editor of the Victor, Colo., *Daily Record.* Then, at 20, he headed for Denver, where he could combine journalism with education.

The University of Denver wouldn't recognize his two degrees, so Thomas put in a combined freshman-sophomore-junior-senior year and got the degrees all over again. Then he moved on to Chicago, entered Kent College of Law, a night school, and found a daytime newspaper job on the Chicago *Journal.*

Newspapermen make friends easily, and Thomas made them in the right places. The high point of his Chicago newspaper career was his exposé of a notorious swindler who had tried to blackmail a number of Chicago meat packers—the Armours, Swifts, Wilson and Cudahys. The Thomas exposé saved them a few million dollars. Those grateful millionaires were to come in handy a few years later.

Thomas couldn't get away from public speaking, but now he was on the listening end. If an underpaid reporter played his cards right, he could wangle a banquet assignment and dine free every night. Thomas did—and found that only one banquet speaker in ten was even passably interesting. He learned what people liked and what bored them; he learned how to start and when to stop, the value of change of pace, the use of light and shade. He also gained about 20 pounds.

Lowell Thomas's first serious brush with travel was curiously linked to his first brush with romance. A former college roommate from Denver dropped in on him in Chicago. The two began recalling their days at the University of Denver.

"Tommy," the friend said, "which girl did you like best?"

"I guess," Thomas said, "Fran Ryan is the loveliest girl I've ever known."

"Did you ever tell her so?" the friend asked.

"No," said Thomas.

"Why don't you?"

Thomas thought about that, and sent Frances Ryan a telegram: Coming to Denver Stop Want to talk to you Stop.

To get to Denver he persuaded some railroad officials that he was the man to write glowingly of the West and San Francisco's coming International Exposition. Denver was a stopover, just long enough to propose to Fran Ryan—and to get turned down.

5

"You didn't even date me, when you were in college!" she said indignantly.

Thomas kept right on going until he reached San Francisco. There he bought a motion-picture camera that weighed almost as much as he did, and set out for Alaska, the Klondike and adventure. He didn't find adventure easily. The tough trails the miners mushed in '98 were now smooth with roads and railroads.

In Whitehorse there were a few old-timers who remembered the days when the more desperate fortune hunters shot Miles Canyon and Whitehorse Rapids in rafts and scows and anything that would hold them. Those who told the stories had made it; many others hadn't.

Thomas needled one survivor into trying it again. They dug up a 12-foot skiff and started down the Yukon. They shot Miles Canyon and then hit Whitehorse Rapids. Thomas was too busy cranking his movie camera to be frightened. Suddenly he looked up. The old man was shaking and, as their craft crashed its way through the rapids, his face was as white as the snow on the mountains beyond. It was then that Thomas's hair began to stand on end. At that moment, he believes, the adventurer in him was born.

He entered Princeton in 1914 to study constitutional law, became a part-time instructor of public speaking, and began to think seriously about an academic career. But on week-ends he showed his movies and talked on Alaska to church groups and women's clubs. He soon realized that he could make more money in two or three days on the platform than a college professor made in a whole month.

The next summer he was off to Alaska again to make more movies. Meanwhile, he pelted Fran Ryan with letters without getting an answer. On the way home he decided to stop in Colorado long enough to see her—and in Arizona to see the Grand Canyon. There he met a cowboy who offered to show him how the early Mormon settlers crossed the turbulent Colorado River by cable.

The cable was still there, but the cage in which the Mormons had made the crossing was no longer in use. That didn't stop the cowboy. He slung some wires over the cable and attached a small board. Sitting on the board, he and Thomas pulled themselves across, hand over hand, 200 feet above one of the most dangerous rivers in the world.

"That rusty old cable," says Thomas, rubbing his hands reminiscently, "was just like barbed wire. With gloves it would have been all right—but who carried gloves?"

World War I had started, and Europe was off-limits to American tourists. Franklin K. Lane, Secretary of the Interior, decided that this would be a dandy time for everyone to "See America First." He called a meeting in Washington to devise a high-powered campaign to back up the slogan.

"They tell me there's a Professor Thomas at Princeton who is getting people all stirred up about Alaska with movies and eloquence," someone reported to Secretary Lane. "Why don't you ask him to spread himself a bit and get them to See America First?"

They sent for Thomas and gave him the job. But by the time he got back to Princeton to resign, the United States was in the First World War and the "See America First" campaign was in limbo. Nevertheless, Professor Thomas had sold himself thoroughly.

"Go on over to Europe," Secretary Lane told him. "Take a look at the war and come back and tell Americans what we're up against. The people don't know."

Lane got permission from President Wilson and Secretary of War Newton D. Baker for Thomas to go everywhere, to see, photograph and write what he wanted. There was just one stumbling block —the cost of the expedition, a little matter of $100,000. Congress was in a recalcitrant mood. Lane didn't dare ask for the appropriation.

"Do you suppose *you* could raise $100,000?" he asked the 25-year-old Thomas.

Thomas didn't even have enough to get married on, a matter which he thought more important. But then he remembered those grateful meat packers in Chicago who had said, "If there is ever anything we can do for you . . ."

He went to Chicago and presented his problem to the heads of the great packing companies. They rounded up 18 multimillionaires, who then rounded up the $100,000. Thomas caught a train for Denver and married Fran.

World War I was, among other things, their honeymoon. Lowell went dashing off to this front and that. Fran joined the Red Cross. They might have had more time together if Lowell hadn't been such a good reporter. One night in Venice, just after he had returned from a rough tour of the Italian front, he saw a military bulletin fastened to the sandbags in front of St. Mark's. It said that Gen. Sir Edmund H. H. Allenby had been assigned to command the British forces in Egypt.

Thomas knew that if the great Allenby was being sent to the Near East, something big must be in the air.

Lowell began pulling every wire he could find to get to Egypt. He sent a thousand-word telegram to the British Foreign Office. Knowing the propaganda value of good news coverage, the British welcomed the idea Thomas offered and dispatched a destroyer to Taranto to take him and Harry Chase, his photographer, to Egypt.

The Palestine campaign was historic. For more than a thousand years Christian crusaders had tried to wrest the Holy Land from the Moslems and had failed. Thomas covered that amazing campaign— a military masterpiece, in which General Allenby captured Jerusalem without firing a shot at the Holy City.

Thomas paused in Jerusalem to catch his breath before going back to the European war. One day he was haggling with an Arab merchant over the price of a pound of dates when a group of Arabs approached. They were tall, tawny, bearded Bedouins—all except one of them.

Lowell was startled by the sight of this short, slender young man wearing Arab robes and headdress. He was light-haired, blue-eyed and beardless. By the time Thomas recovered from his astonishment, the Arabs and the blond Bedouin had disappeared.

Inquiry led him to Sir Ronald Storrs, the governor of the Holy City. Storrs walked to a door leading from his office to an inner room and threw it open. There sat the blond "Arab"—Col. Thomas Edward Lawrence, the scholarly young British archeologist who was rejected for military service at the start of the war but who in the end won a famous victory. And thus began one of the great stories of our time: Lowell Thomas's story of Lawrence of Arabia.

Joining the British Secret Service, Lawrence had asked to be sent into Arabia. He knew that unrest was smoldering against the Turks (who were threatening the Suez Canal and all of Egypt). Dressed in Arab garb, Lawrence made his way to the camp of young Feisal, ablest of the Arab rebels, won his confidence, and planned and executed one of the most brilliantly daring campaigns in military history. His uncanny strategy helped demoralize the Turks and bring about the fall of Damascus and the old Turkish Empire.

Lowell Thomas won Lawrence's confidence as completely as Lawrence had won Feisal's. He returned with Lawrence to Arabia, put on Arab garb himself and, with Harry Chase and his motion-picture camera, covered the climax of the campaign and the conquest. Then Thomas hurried back to catch up with the European war. What he caught up with was the Armistice.

Now the big question was: "What's going on inside Germany?" Every newspaper correspondent in Europe wanted to get there and find out. Three of them did get as far as Berlin. But before they could sharpen their pencils Gen. "Black Jack" Pershing had them picked up by the scruffs of their necks and tossed out.

Thomas bet Webb Waldron of *Collier's* that he could get into Germany, Waldron went along to make sure he collected if he won. One night they were sitting in a rathskeller in Mulhouse, France, when they noticed a man in a French uniform who was obviously an American. He was full of despair and French wine.

It seems he had a nice new ambulance, but the war was over and all that was left for him to do was pick up stragglers coming out of Germany. Thomas asked him whether he would care to help a couple of stragglers straggle the other way—*into* Germany. The driver liked that idea, told them to get in the ambulance and lie down on the floor. Then he piled stretchers and blankets over them. Away they went.

Once they reached Germany no one paid any attention to them. They got to Berlin while the rebellion was still going on and the Socialists were shooting it out with the Spartacists. Thomas got shot —through the hat, fortunately, not the head.

They got back to Paris in time for the peace conference. Thomas and Waldron gave President Wilson the first late news he'd had from inside Germany. As a reward they were sent home aboard the *Leviathan*—in what had once been the Kaiser's imperial suite.

Thomas came back eager to talk about the war but found that nobody wanted to listen. The war was over and it had been "the war to end all wars" and that was that.

But after any war, people do want to be entertained. Thomas had long had a theory that people didn't want to hear lectures; they wanted to see "shows." So he took over the Century Theatre in New York and gave them shows—colorful, dramatic stories of the war itself, the American soldiers in France, the German revolution, the

Egyptian campaign and the Arabian defeat of the Turks, all illustrated by motion pictures.

People began flocking to see and hear. He moved into Madison Square Garden. He narrowed his "shows" down to two subjects: the great crusade which conquered Jerusalem, after a thousand years under Turkish rule, led by a giant of a man, General Allenby; and the fight of the Arabs to regain their national identity, led by a 5 foot 3 inch Englishman, Lawrence of Arabia. Thomas played for 12 weeks in New York—an unheard-of run.

On the last night Percy Burton, a British impresario, dropped in to see what was drawing such huge crowds. The subject that night was Lawrence of Arabia. Burton made his way backstage at the conclusion of the show. He had been held spellbound, hearing an American tell a fascinating story of a fabulous British hero of whom he, a Briton, had never heard. He insisted that Thomas must appear in London.

"All right," said Thomas. "If you can get me an invitation from the King and put me on at Covent Garden Royal Opera House, I'll go." That settled that, he thought. Covent Garden was the traditional home of the opera, and the King didn't invite unknown Americans to speak in London.

Two weeks later Burton cabled that he had booked Covent Garden. A week after that came an invitation from King George V.

Thomas really went to work on his "show." He combined the Allenby and Lawrence talks into one. He began the proceedings with the first movie prologue in history—slinky moonlight-on-the-Nile music and a seven-veil dance. Then, for good measure, he tossed in the Royal Welsh Guards Band in their blazing uniforms. He knocked London for a dignified British loop.

What started out as a two-week engagement kept the opera out of Covent Garden for a month. Eventually Thomas moved to Albert Hall. Crowned heads, and some that deserved crowns, came by the aisleful—the King and Queen, the Prince of Wales, Lloyd George, Winston Churchill, Clemenceau, Israel Zangwill, Bernard Shaw, Allenby himself and even the shy T. E. Lawrence.

Thomas postponed a scheduled American tour and toured the world instead, giving his show more than 2000 times under all sorts of conditions. In Ceylon there was no roof, and monkeys dropped coconuts on the customers. In Malaya the lights attracted bats almost as big as eagles.

Thomas found India "the greatest human show on earth." So when he finished he went back to put it on film. He ran into politics and red tape and finally took his case to the Viceroy, Lord Reading. "You can have anything you want in India," said the Viceroy. "Just name it."

"I would like special trains when I need them, and the use of the Indian army occasionally."

Lord Reading didn't bat an eye, Thomas got what he asked for, including an army officer "who can speak as many languages as possible." The Indian tour took two years and included Burma, Afghanistan and Malaya. When it was over, Thomas persuaded the army officer to resign and write a book. The man was Francis Yeats-Brown—the book, *Lives of a Bengal Lancer.* It made history of its own as a best-seller and a motion picture.

Thomas came out with two shows and a cast of a million people, all told. He took these shows to Paris and London, then came back to America and picked up his long-delayed tour, playing almost every town in the country with more than 5000 people. When it was finished he was so satiated with seas of faces and the sound of his own voice that he resolved never again to appear before audiences.

He had traveled thousands of miles in the last six years. He had been around the world. Now he didn't want to budge an inch. He wanted the quietest life he could find. He wanted rural peace and seclusion. He wanted to write, not to talk. He and Fran looked for a place to settle down. They found what they wanted in New York's Dutchess County, a 500-acre farm on Quaker Hill, Pawling. They went deeply into debt and bought it.

Now Lowell had to go to work in earnest. He called on Russell Doubleday to sell him an unwritten book. Before he left Doubleday's office he had sold six unwritten books and had in his pocket a check for the largest advance royalty ever paid to a writer up to that time. Thomas didn't stop with those six books. He kept right on going. Since then he has written 40 more.

In the meantime, something new had been added to the world of words. It touched Thomas first, and inconspicuously, in London in October 1923, at the time his son, Lowell, Jr., was born.

One day Thomas went to the nursing home to see his wife and baby, and found Harry Chase, his cameraman, sitting in the room

11

holding a small box, and wearing "ear muffs" and a concentrated look. He handed the "ear muffs" to Thomas who put them on and heard a voice he recognized. It was Lord Curzon talking about India in the House of Lords—several miles away. The box was a crystal-set radio.

Thomas marveled at the gadget, but it never occurred to him that radio would boom and mushroom until it became his pet aversion. It soon interfered with his work and his social life. It reached the point where a guest, arriving at Thomas's Quaker Hill home, would stand in the doorway and say, "I won't come in unless you promise not to serve dinner until after 'Amos and Andy.' "

It was always Mrs. Thomas who said, "Come on in!" Lowell was furious about the whole radio business.

But, in spite of his own wishes, radio kept on booming and growing—music, entertainment and, inevitably, news. One day in 1930, when Thomas was at home writing a couple of books, the telephone rang.

"You don't know me," said the voice at the other end, "but I'm one of the executives of the Columbia Broadcasting Company [it was a mere company at that time], and I'm about to lose my job! I heard you speak in London, and I believe you're the only man in the world who can save my job for me. Meet me in the city at 52nd and Madison as soon as you can. When you get here, I'll tell you about it."

That is still the quickest way to get Thomas anywhere. Make it mysterious and you've got him. He met his man, who took him to the office of William Paley, a young Philadelphian who had recently bought what is now CBS. Paley put Thomas in front of a microphone.

"When you hear the buzzer," Paley said, "start talking."

"What about?" asked Thomas.

"Anything. Talk 15 minutes. Then stop."

Paley left the room. Thomas looked around and saw three standby musicians. "When I start talking, you start playing," he told them. "Play anything, just so it's sort of Oriental."

The buzzer buzzed. Thomas started talking. The musicians played dreamy music. Thomas talked of adventures in India, told stories of pygmies in Malaya, described mysterious ceremonies in Afghanistan. In 15 minutes Paley came and escorted Thomas into another room where he faced the now traditional ogres of broadcasting—the sponsors. There were 20 of them, all officials of Funk & Wagnalls, publishers of *Literary Digest.* Theirs was the only daily news broadcast at the time.

The sponsors said they liked Thomas but wanted to hear him do a news program. Would he come back again? It was Paley who said he would indeed. The Funk & Wagnalls program was then on the National Broadcasting Co. network. If Columbia could get the program away from NBC, it meant a million-dollar triumph.

The day was set. At nine o'clock in the morning the assembling of a script began. Paley had called in writers and trouble-shooters, Thomas's publishers had called in more writers, and Thomas himself had assembled some. Everybody had a different idea of what should be done.

By four o'clock, Thomas couldn't stand the confusion. He walked out, bought an evening newspaper, came back at six o'clock, stepped up to the microphone and said simply, "Good evening, everybody," and told the news. When he had finished he said, just as simply, "So long until tomorrow." He got the contract.

Thomas has been broadcasting the news every weekday since— 31 years, the longest continuous daily broadcast in the history of radio. He smiled a little smile of his own a few years ago when "Amos and Andy" went off the air and the endurance record passed to him.

Lowell Thomas and radio were invented for each other. Of course Thomas was invented first, so he brought a great deal to the new medium. There was all his father's work back in Cripple Creek, which made every syllable clear and audible as far as air waves could reach. There were the years of experience on the platform and the years of travel to practically every corner of the globe, which gave him an insight into people and places. Then there was his voice, with its resonant timbre, which for years has been the despair of rivals.

Soon his "Good evening, everybody" meant just that to almost everybody who owned a radio. There is no way of estimating accurately the number of ears that have tuned in on him, but the most conservative guess would be astronomical.

He has broadcast from mountain-tops, from the depths of mines, from ships at sea, from airplanes. Once, on the island of Luzon in the Philippines during the war, he set up his microphone in a tomb underground. One well-placed shot and he might have joined the occupant.

He broadcasts the news, all the news and nothing but the news. When it comes to the expression of opinion he is as noncommittal as the microphone itself. He takes no sides. He never analyzes, never makes profound pronouncements, delivers no messages, sounds no alarms. Even his best friends do not always know where he stands politically.

Through radio Thomas became a disembodied voice. But it wasn't long before the disembodied voice of radio had a body. Fox Movietone News signed him to do their newsreel commentary. He spoke before their cameras for 17 years.

When TV came along, Thomas was chosen to do its first news telecast. But he decided quickly that TV news was not for him, and stayed with radio.

"They want to hear the news, not see the person who is reading it," he says. "No one wants to see the same fellow on the screen every day unless he happens to look like Michelangelo's David," Which is difficult to do with your clothes on.

When Cinerama came along, Hollywood didn't know what to do with three-dimensional photography. But Thomas had been living a three-dimensional life for years. In a few months he was up to his neck in Cinerama. He had always wanted to revise the list of the "Seven Wonders of the World," which was 2000 years old. His Cinerama film of the new Seven Wonders and his wide-screen film, "The Search for Paradise," and the first one, "This Is Cinerama," were a revelation. They took people to places where they could never set foot.

Thomas had scorned television at its start but it finally engulfed him—at least temporarily—in 1957, when he started on a series called "High Adventure." This involved 11 breath-taking expeditions. The first was among the cannibals of New Guinea, a tribe which had just eaten 35 members of a rival tribe at a little dinner party. The second was to the North Pole. The others covered the world from Madagascar to Timbuktu, from the Himalayas to the Australian desert, from Africa's Mountains of the Moon to Alaska.

The show that topped them all, however, was the color film of an expedition Lowell Thomas, Sr., and Lowell Thomas, Jr., had

14

made into the forbidden land of Tibet in 1949.

In Tibet the Thomases met—and filmed for the first time—the Dalai Lama, young ruler of this strange country who since has been forced to flee from the conquering Chinese Reds to India. Thomas was the seventh American and his son the eighth ever to reach Lhasa, the mystery-shrouded capital of the kingdom in the Himalayan clouds.

The expedition was on its way out of Tibet when Thomas was thrown by his horse on a remote mountain pass. His hip was broken in eight places. In a land which does not believe in doctors, and at an altitude where oxygen is thin, Thomas's life was in danger every moment. In Tibet no airplanes, no cars, no carts, no bicycles were allowed. For twenty days he was carried over rocky trails, suffering intense pain all the way. He was on crutches for months, but before a year passed he was skiing on the Juneau Ice Cap in Alaska.

Skiing, incidentally, has played quite a part in the life of Lowell Thomas—and, on the other hand, Lowell Thomas has played quite a part in the life of skiing. He first met the sport in the Italian Alps in World War I. But it was the 1932 Winter Olympic Games at Lake Placid, N. Y., that turned him into a zealot.

Since then he has encouraged the building of ski slopes in Vermont, New Hampshire, Maine, Colorado, and at Mt. Tremblant in Canada. On his 50th birthday he went over the Headwall at Tuckerman's Ravine, N. H., a 1000-foot sheer precipice.

If it's snowing and there's a slope around, Thomas can't wait to get on his skis. Maynard Miller, the geologist, recalls that when he and Thomas were on an expedition in Alaska in 1950, a tiny plane landed at their camp with supplies. The next thing Miller saw was Lowell—heading for the plane—on skis. The plane took off and flew to the top of a nearby mountain, 6000 feet high. A few minutes later, Lowell came skiing down. The mountain must have looked pretty surprised.

Golf is a milder passion. He has played it in every part of the world. He also took up softball, in a celebrity-studded way, organizing a team known as the "Nine Old Men," which at times included such luminaries as Eddie Rickenbacker, Gene Tunney, John Kieran, Colonel Stoopnagle, Jack Dempsey, Dale Carnegie, Lanny Ross and Thomas E. Dewey. Their "big" games were against a team managed by Franklin D. Roosevelt.

15

At 69, Lowell Thomas stands as straight as the shortest distance between two points. His hair is still thick, chestnut-brown and curly. For a fellow who has been everywhere and dined on everything from blubber to blueberries, he is neither a gourmet nor a fastidious eater. But he denies that everything tastes like ham and eggs to him.

He's a fanatic on orderliness. He would walk into a room in Buckingham Palace and straighten a picture on the wall if it was hanging on the bias. He has done more good turns than a rotary broiler. He has a memory that would make an elephant seem absent-minded. He still likes to dance, swim, ride, golf and ski—and there are times when he seems to be doing all of them at the same time.

Thomas is the only person who has refused to submit meekly to the tear-jerking formula of Ralph Edwards' TV program "This Is Your Life." The carefully rehearsed background of the show was planned, as usual, to catch the "star" by surprise. Thomas was trapped at a public dinner. Suddenly the floodlights flashed on, Edwards rushed to the dais, microphone in hand, and announced, "Lowell Thomas, *this* is your life!" Lowell gritted his teeth audibly. "This," he growled, "is a sinister conspiracy." The ensuing goings-on were both topsy and turvy. They also made television history.

Thomas recognized the offstage voice of his sister, Pherbia Thomas Thornburg, saying, "Father insisted that you learn every rock and mineral in that mining camp." He snorted, "I also knew every saloon in Cripple Creek." Edwards gasped and rushed Fran Thomas onstage. While he sentimentalized the story of their courtship, Fran whispered in Lowell's ear.

"Want to know what she said?" blurted out Thomas. "She said, '*Must* I kiss you here?' "

Lowell's brilliant, roly-poly editor, the late Prosper Buranelli, recited his set piece, grinned at his dour-faced boss and asked, "How mad are you?"

"Prosper," Thomas said sternly, "you've had too much to drink."

"Too much?" Buranelli retorted. "Not enough!"

By this time everything but the camera was out of focus. Cues were missed, commercials forgotten, Edwards bobbed about on a sea of nerves and the show ran overtime. But the TV audience loved it. The next night on his own broadcast Thomas explained sheepishly, "If I seemed a bit sardonic, it was because I was utterly startled." Ralph Edwards wasn't sheepish but ecstatic when he saw the program's rating for that evening—an all-time high. "Lowell Thomas was the best thing that ever happened to us," he said. "I'm going to submit the show to the TV academy as the best comedy of the season."

Today Thomas leads what might be called for him a quiet life. Quaker Hill has become a thriving community. In a Georgian mansion of 40 rooms he presides as a happy squire over an estate with a golf course, a ski run, a lake, a swimming pool, a tennis court, a baseball diamond and a radio station, among other things.

He probably knows more people than any other man alive. When the telephone rings at Quaker Hill, the caller could be Queen Elizabeth, Grandma Moses, Jack Kennedy, Helen Hayes, Jimmy Doolittle, General de Gaulle, Prince Rainier, the Dalai Lama, Herbert Hoover, Haile Selassie, Bennett Cerf, the Aga Khan, Zsa Zsa Gabor, Elvis Presley, Ernest Hemingway or Santa Claus.

What's left to see for a man who has seen everything and who has been everywhere? What about outer space?

"The nearest planet outside our own solar system is four billion miles away," says Lowell. "No one knows whether it is inhabited. I like people. Now, if they ever find an inhabited planet . . ." And his eyes look out vaguely at something four light-years distant.

Perhaps when that telephone at Quaker Hill rings some night it may be Lowell Thomas himself: "Hello, Fran. This is Lowell. I won't be home for dinner. No, don't wait for me. I'm leaving in ten minutes for Mars."

And then, finally, out of sheer force of habit: "So long until tomorrow!"

Birthplace of L.T. at Woodington, in Darke County, Ohio. Annie Oakley was born "around the corner."

Lowell Thomas addition to Garst Museum, Darke County Historical Society, in Greenville, presented to the community by Fred Coppock, a Darke County philanthropist.

At age 8, with his mother, Harriet Wagner Thomas. She was a teacher, as was his father before becoming an M.D. Picture taken in Greenville, Ohio, Darke County.

In the summer of 1907, Lowell and his parents journeyed back to Greenville, for a family reunion. His parents are on the extreme left. Lowell is in the right rear, arrow. Age 15.

Dr. Harry George Thomas was an erudite man of many interests who ignored the calendar. Every few years he would take refresher courses at Universities, both at home and abroad. His final fling was at age 83 when he headed for Oxford and further graduate study.

Long before the U.S. entered World War 1 in 1917, he had become an officer in the British Army.

In 1918 Lowell, already influential with U.S. Army headquarters despite his years (25) because of his war coverage, suggested to General Ireland and General Pershing that it might not be a bad idea to transfer some Americans already serving with other armies to the American Expeditionary Force and, thereby, benefit from their experience.

This was done. And that was how his father became a Colonel in the A.E.F., although he never knew it was due to his son.

Lowell's father, 1900, Victor, Colorado. A man with a keen and inquisitive mind. Dr. Thomas drilled his son in the art of public speaking as well as in the arts and sciences. Among other things, he taught geology and astronomy on long hikes in the Rockies.

Lowell (circled) in the Fifth Grade of Garfield School at Victor, the year 1902, when he was already earning money selling newspapers in the local saloons.

Interest in sports came early. A member of the High School football team of 1908 at age 16, playing end and quarterback. Second from right, second row from front.

This is Victor, Colorado, heart of the Cripple Creek mining district, 1900.

Panoramic view of Victor, when gold mines were booming. Portland No. 1 and No. 2

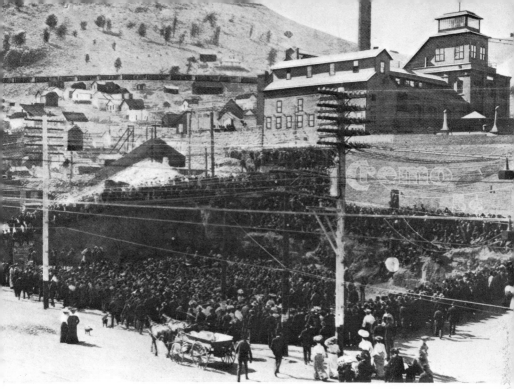

Gunfire erupted at a mass meeting of miners on June 6, 1904, in a riot over the IWW union issue in front of Vindicator mine. Sixteen were killed. Young Lowell, age 13, looked on from father's nearby office, until told to lie on floor. His father treated victims and received one lone six-shooter and holster as his only pay.

In 1907, an unusual job, riding 9 hours a day for an assay office, collecting samples from small mines; then returning next day—usually with sad news.

Whizzing through the University of Northern Indiana (Valparaiso) in two years, he collected a B.S. and an M.S. Making friends with daughters of two professors may have helped!

During the summer of 1912, Lowell in the role of cowpuncher on his father's ranch near Four Corners area of Colorado, New Mexico, Utah and Arizona.

His first job after college—a pick and shovel miner, sometimes 1,000 feet underground. Pay $3 a day—30 days a month. Sorry, no days off.

Soon he was offered a job at $95 a month as a reporter on the *Victor Daily Record,* and then editor, with sister Pherbia. Later he became editor of a rival paper, the *Daily News,* and at age 19 was telling neighbors how to vote before eligible to vote himself.

1912, age 20, still wearing his Cripple Creek "Stetson" he left Victor for Chicago and law school. Dressed like this, he walked into the office of the *Chicago Journal* (now the *Sun-Times*), and famed city editor Richard J. Finnegan said to an associate: "If that young man wants a job, he's got one." Lowell did; he did. Lowell chased fires and from 7 a.m. to 5 p.m. associated with legendary Chicago reporters Ben Hecht, Charles MacArthur, Floyd Gibbons, Carl Sandburg, Ring Lardner, studied law at night.

Checking war devastation on Italian front, he talks with Italian woman in destroyed home just back of front lines.

During World War I, with General Pepino Garibaldi, son of the Italian liberator. Time: 1917. Place: Zenzon Bridgehead on the Piave River.

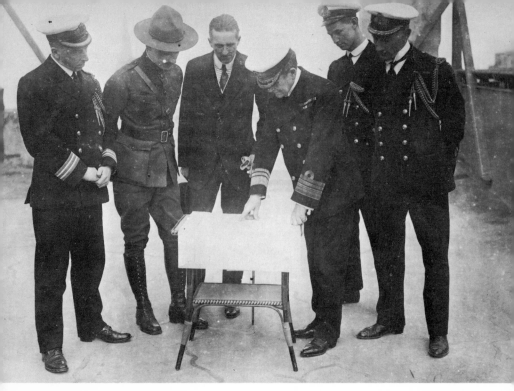

En route to Palestine, L.T.'s ship was chased into Malta harbor by U-Boat. Admiral Lord Calthorpe, Second British Sea Lord, briefs group including Lt. Cdr. Charles Dickens, right, grandson of famous British novelist.

Driving down the old Jericho Road from Jerusalem to the Jordan—the same route taken by the Good Samaritan. L.T. in turret of early-day armored car.

SECTION 2

All journalists are alert to the "big story," the exclusive drama which can be theirs alone and make them famous overnight.

One of the most sensational "big stories" of this century was broken at the end of World War I by a young American foreign correspondent. Age 25, he was fresh out of law school and Princeton.

The story? Lawrence of Arabia. By Lowell Thomas.

Lowell was the first journalist to appreciate the full significance of the strategy of General Sir Edmund H. H. Allenby, and was the only observer in Arabia with T. E. Lawrence. He sought them out and told their story to the world. The rest is history. Walter Duranty, long Moscow correspondent for The New York Times, *and one of the most brilliant of all foreign correspondents said that his colleague had pulled off one of the greatest journalistic "scoops" of all time.*

After the war, Lowell put together a film-illustrated presentation on the war, the Campaigns of Allenby of Jerusalem and Lawrence of Arabia. He scored an unusual success in New York City, packing the Century Theater and Madison Square Garden for 12 weeks—a record.

But that success was just a mild preview, relatively, of things to come. England was the homeland of Allenby and Lawrence.

A noted impressario, Percy Burton, urged Lowell to bring his presentation to London. Lowell jokingly agreed, providing he was invited by the King and launched at Covent Garden Royal Opera House. Those conditions met, Lowell sailed for England.

To properly present his story, he created a new entertainment form, "the live film prologue."

What it was, and what it did are related in the following two articles, the first by Capt. Alan Bott, English author and London editor of "The World's Work," and the second by author-editor Gove Hambidge.

A Yankee Captures London

By CAPT. ALAN BOTT, M.C.R.A.F. *English author of "Eastern Nights"*

One of the strangest sights in London since the war was the large crowd that gathered twice daily before the doors of the Royal Opera House, Covent Garden. The door being opened, it filled every seat in the famous theatre. And the attraction? An American troubadour talking on a war subject!

London, like the rest of Great Britain, has never acquired the lecture habit. It is as a rule too reserved, aloof and unenthusiastic to sit still for two hours, merely for the interest of coming into direct contact with a personality. Moreover, it does not care overmuch for information in tabloid form. Many men have discovered this. So when I heard of Lowell Thomas' intention to visit London, I thought I should be acting in unfriendly manner if I refrained from advising him to forget it. But he persisted, backed by the vision of Percy Burton, for many years manager to Henry Irving and Forbes-Robertson. The English-Speaking Union of London, which aims at promoting friendship between all English-speaking people, realizing the value of a visit from Lowell Thomas, added its quota of persuasion.

The gloom prophets, including myself, were influenced largely in their predictions of woeful failure by the fact that Lowell Thomas' narrative, and the motion pictures that illustrate it, dealt largely with the war—albeit with the two most romantic and least known aspects of the war, the campaigns in Palestine and Arabia.

Mr. Burton went to London and found that the only vacant theatre was the great Opera House in Covent Garden, one of the best-known theatres in the world. The lessees, while believing Lowell Thomas and Percy Burton to be smitten with insanity, were willing enough to rent their property until the next opera season opened in the late Fall. A good-intentioned warning was offered, however, by Sir Thomas Beecham. "My dear Sirs," said he, "you stand no more chance than a snow-ball in the Jordan Valley." Sir Thomas Beecham, like myself, attended Lowell Thomas' first Lon-

don appearance; and like myself, he apologized for having been a
false prophet of woe.

The subject was "WITH ALLENBY IN PALESTINE AND
LAWRENCE IN ARABIA." To me, as an aviator who had flown in
the Palestine Campaign, the evening was of special interest; and I
was one of a party of British officers who had served under General
Allenby. We did not expect much from the speaker. What could a
mere war observer—one of a tribe that, though living on the fringe
of the battlefields, as a rule failed utterly to catch the spirit and
subtle outlook of the fighting men, and dished up for the benefit of
unsuspecting civilians a sentimental mess of garbled verbiage—re-
veal of this greatest of all the campaigns in the long history of the
Holy Land? We came, in fact, to scoff indulgently—but we remained
to clap, hard.

I lived again through many fantastic · days and nights of cam-
paigning among and flying above the deserts, the bleak hill-country,
and the vivid towns of Judea, Samaria, Sinai and Syria, while the
changing-film-tapestry flickered across the screen, to the accompani-
ment of Lowell Thomas' explanations. He showed me my own air-
drome among the Jaffa orange groves. He showed pictures from the
air of his flight from Cairo to Jerusalem. Gaza, where Samson's
prowess was equalled by Allenby's—Beersheba, where the Scotsmen,
Australians and Bikinir Camel Corps drove the Turks from the home
of Abraham—Ramleh, where Allenby had his head-quarters, as for a
time did Napoleon—Nebi Samwill hill, whence Richard Coeur de
Lion looked with longing eyes at the Holy City he never entered,
and to capture which many a Tommy, Anzac, Irishman, Welshman,
Ghurka and Scotty laid down his life, thus paving the way for the
regiments which marched solemnly into Jerusalem—these and many
other places with magic names were pictured and described exactly
as they appeared to us, when we fought around and entered into
them. Indian Lancers, Australian Light Horse, Egyptian Camel
Corps, Tommies in "shorts," Bedouin irregulars of the desert, flying
men who were my companions, all passed in vivid review across the
screen, amid surroundings that brought back to me the gorgeous
colour, the vivid sunlight, the pungent smells, the glorious sights of
the Near East that hotel tourists do not see.

And then, the American speaker's illustrated story of the modern
Arabian Nights, a fantastic and unbelievably romantic tale that was

31

kept secret during the war, and even now would never have been told but for Lowell Thomas, the only person who went into the forbidden deserts of holy Arabia and ate dates and drank camels milk with mystery man, Lawrence, who by personal bravery and by brilliant diplomacy accomplished in a few months what Sultans and statesmen of the Near East failed to do in the past eight hundred years.

Can you beat this historical fact with fictional romance? Evidently the huge audiences at the Royal Opera House could not; for, as Lowell Thomas described in breath-taking detail the life of Thomas Lawrence, "the uncrowned king of Arabia," he seemed to be, not a lecturer talking through the nose of a Yankee" (his own words), but a latter-day troubadour, telling wonderfully a most wonderful tale. The enthusiasm of the audiences that packed every seat in the Opera House was reflected in the London press notices which abounded with superlatives.

From then onward the success of the Lowell Thomas season was assured. It had caught England's imagination. It was one of those unexplicable achievements of merit that no amount of publicity could have won. From all parts of England, Scotland and Wales people who intended to make special trips to London to see and hear Lowell Thomas sent requests for tickets. Headmasters of schools booked hundreds of seats en bloc. Box parties were given by some of the most prominent people in England, including the Royal families of Britain, Spain, Norway and Arabia, Lloyd George and the members of his cabinet as well as members of both houses of Parliament, Government officials, bishops, Jewish shop-keepers, generals and privates mingled in the audiences. Thousands stood in line for from 8 to 10 hours in fog and rain, and thousands were turned away at a single matinee when special police reserves had to be called from Bow Street. Well-known personalities, including that outstanding figure of intellectual womanhood, Lady Mackenzie, wrote articles in praise of the American's talk and pictures. Blackwood's Magazine referred to it as a brilliant entertainment, and The Strand Magazine called it "the greatest romance of real life ever told." All of the newspapers were filled with columns of lavish praise. A great public banquet at the Criterion Restaurant, arranged by Lord Northcliffe, John Jacob Astor, and others, and presided over by Viscount Burnham, was given in honour of Mr. Thomas.

Lord Burnham referred to him as "a great artist, a ripe scholar, a brave man, and a true friend. As I looked and listened" said the noted publisher, "I felt myself transported off to the East on a magic carpet. This production is an elevation of art as well as a revelation of romance. Lowell Thomas has almost created a new art."

Then came a succession of visits from the chief actors in the great drama, Lieut. General Sir Philip Chetwode, commander of the army that captured Jerusalem, sent congratulations to the speaker's dressing room. Thomas Lawrence—thirty-year-old archaeologist, "uncrowned king of Arabia" and the most romantic figure of his day—bought a ticket one evening, slipped into the house in his usual silent and solitary manner. Prince Feisal (now "King of Bagdad"), one of the great figures in the present-day Arab world, came with his flowing-robed suite of Arab dignitaries, only a day or two after his arrival in London from Damascus. Soon afterwards Field Marshall Viscount Allenby himself, returned from the Near East and was given a magnificent ovation by the London crowds, when he with Lady Allenby and a party of friends came to Covent Garden. Finally Mr. Lowell Thomas received that hall-mark of success—a special request that he should appear at Balmoral Castle before the King and Queen.

This was the first motion picture production that Rudyard Kipling ever saw. In fact Lowell Thomas' dressing room became a rendezvous for celebrities—Tetrazzini, Melba, Israel Zangwill, the Bishop of Jerusalem, Forbes-Robertson, and hosts of others.

Although Lowell Thomas had expected that a fortnight's run in London would be the limit, lo! wonder of wonders, the London opera season—the sacred, ultra fashionable opera season—was postponed so the American might continue. Then from Covent Garden he finally moved to Royal Albert Hall, that colossal white elephant seating 12,000 people, where he again packed the house both afternoon and evening for the longest period in its history of fifty odd years, and where he spoke to 20,000 people daily. On the final night of his historic run, Lord Charnwood, biographer of Lincoln and Roosevelt presented Lowell Thomas with a laurel wreath and the thanks of the public for his great achievement. Then after a tour of the Provinces, the Commonwealth Government cabled, inviting him to tour Australia, and this was followed by a world tour.

But let not other speakers from any clime pack their grips in a hurry and apply for a British visa to their passports, unless they, too, have a story glorious as the exploits of Lord Allenby of Palestine and Thomas Lawrence of Arabia, and can talk as well as Lowell Thomas of America.

Cartooned in London when he presented his "With Lawrence in Arabia and Allenby in Palestine." (Note resemblance to actor who came later—Clark Gable.)

With Field Marshal Allenby, center, and His Royal Highness, the Duke of Connaught (son of Queen Victoria), left, after the fall of Jerusalem.

A meeting with Arab leaders. Left, General Nuri Sa'id, after the War 14 times Prime Minister of Iraq before assassination. In shade, Auda Abu Tayi, paramount Sheikh of the Howeitat Tribe, and Shereef Feisal, later King of Syria and then of Iraq. L.T. at right.

Gonzalez Studi

Behind the Turkish lines, an unknown young Englishman was helping the Arabs throw off centuries of domination while aiding the Allied cause. Lowell "discovered" T. E. Lawrence amid desert sands and told his story to the world. One of the most dramatic stories of the century, it catapulted both to world prominence.

The foreign correspondent in the Holy Land in 1919 traveled rather heavy. Here with Sudanese assistant checking day's work. Luckily he had sensed drama in Allenby's assignment to recapture of the Holy Land that had been under Moslem domination since Middle Ages.

He Was With Lawrence in Arabia

By GOVE HAMBIDGE *Author and Editor* (1928)

The Royal Opera House, Covent Garden, London. A sixty-piece orchestra playing exotic Oriental airs. Out before the rich Oriental stage-setting steps a dancer, twists her body into strange postures. Off-stage a voice softly intones the Mahometan call to prayer: La ilahu illa Allah! Allahu Akbar! A silver-screen descends. Before it there walks a lithe, black-haired young man. . . .

Suddenly a troop of mad-riding burnous-clad Arabs whirls upon the silver-screen. They are a hot-blooded horde under the command of Lawrence, poet, archaeologist, soldier, "uncrowned King of Arabia." The young man before the screen begins to talk. Step by step he unfolds the strange drama of Lawrence's Arabian campaign, hitherto unknown to the world, and which he was among the few outsiders to witness. His words are timed perfectly to suit the action upon the screen. His deep, trained voice moves that audience now to bursts of laughter, now to sharp, emotional shocks.

When he has finished, a wind of handclapping sweeps the open house from pit to gallery. Celebrities hurry backstage to congratulate him—Lloyd George, Venizelos, Tetrazzini, Melba, Zangwill, Forbes-Robertson. The King commands him to appear at Balmoral Castle and tell the tale of Lawrence and Allenby to the assembled royal family. He is feted and dined by peers. Special trains pour in from as far as Wales, loaded with people to hear that epic tale. He is invited to Australia as a guest of the government to tell it; then to Bombay, Calcutta, Rangoon, Singapore and so on around the globe. He makes a triumphal tour of the British Empire. He tells his strange drama *four thousand times, to four million people*, sometimes to twenty thousand a day.

This lithe young man with the very steady blue eyes is Lowell Thomas, author of "Count Luckner the Sea Devil," "With Lawrence in Arabia," "Beyond Khyber Pass." He is a young fellow who sucked romance through the nipple of his nursing bottle.

The world is his oyster, neatly pried open, served up on royal porcelain with plenty of tobasco and horseradish. He is Fate's pet child. He is a twentieth-century skald, singing modern songs of high adventure. He makes his living by stepping up the world's pulse rate. He has more adventures a month than the average man in a lifetime.

Lowell Thomas is the son of a surgeon infected with wanderlust. The echo of the Pike's Peak-or-bust cry was still reverberating through this country when young Thomas was eight. His father carted him from Timbuktu and Kamchatka and the Klondike, carried ore samples from miner to assayer, and got the lust of romance into his blood by listening to a thousand tales of rough-and-ready adventure. He got the smell of printer's ink into his blood, too, working as a printer's devil.

He lived on the top of the world. Every day, from that 10,000-foot eyrie on the rim of an extinct volcano, he looked out over 150 miles of stark, magnificent mountain ranges. "And that got into my blood, too," he said. . . . "But, on the other hand, not far from where I now live, there is an inn. People motor for miles to sip expensive tea and gurgle over the gorgeous view. The place was sold to the inn owners by an old farmer who had pastured cows on that hilltop every day of his life. Years afterward he read about the inn, made famous by its outlook. He hurried back hotfoot to his old home, climbed the hill he had been up and down ten thousand times. 'Gosh!' he said. 'That is a nice view! I never noticed it!' "

Young Thomas was taught to appreciate. With his father, he wore out the knees of his pants climbing up mountain peaks, and their seat sliding down into gorges; he learned the rightful names of stones and flowers and stars; he learned reverence for nature's handiwork. And he learned another, odder thing. With malice aforethought, he was made into a boy orator. From the time he was a toddler of four, his father had him up on the carpet spouting poetry and prose which he had to learn by heart.

Three or four times each week the youngster had to do this—a crazy, amazingly wise procedure. He had to learn to get his voice out of his nose and down where it belonged, to gesture with appropriate elliptical grace, these things became second nature; his father went at the thing as he would go at a surgical job.

"Some day you'll thank me, son," the father said. Young Thomas hated it.

But when he got into high school he nonchalantly pulled off a rip-snorting, man-sized oration one day, made every youngster his friend in a flash, and was elected captain of the football team on the strength of it. Then he knew that the ability to stand on your feet and talk has its good points.

Young Thomas's later education took him to four universities. At Valparaiso he worked his way through. He fed a cow, a furnace, a laundry and his fellow students—the latter as cook and waiter in a quick and dirty. Through his boyhood knowledge of stones he became assistant to the geology professor. Summers he sold maps and real estate. And with all this he flipped off the four-year course in two years.

Back in Cripple Creek, the new-hatched A.B. passed up white-collar jobs and headed for the mines, where he shoveled rock some 1,000 feet down in the earth's intestines. The owner of the local paper lured him away to become a cub reporter. When he had hustled for the paper a year, long enough to get the job of managing editor, he stowed away his white collar and, gripped by wanderlust, made for the Land of the Cliff Dwellers, where he forked a pinto and chased cows. Then he decided to go after more education.

At the University of Denver he bagged another brace of degrees; he is a wing shot when it comes to education. Then he went on to Chicago, with the idea of studying for the noble pursuit of law. He had to earn his way, so he took a job as newspaper reporter, breaking in with a group that was later to become famous—Carl Sandburg, Ben Hecht, Harry Hansen, Mary Synon. He was a reporter from 7 a.m. to 5 p.m., thereafter a student of law. His ability to speak like a veteran criminal prosecutor was spotted at once, and he was taken on as an instructor in forensic oratory. He taught a few thousand older men than himself how to say what was on their minds, "and learned a lot more than I gave," he says.

Two years of this work, and he went out to the Coast to do a set of newspaper articles. But he didn't want to go back when he had finished. There was a lure up yonder, northward; he followed it, and made his debut as a chechahco in Alaska. This was grand and glorious; here was the tang of adventure. He got a scow, shot Miles Canyon and the White Horse Rapids, and then went on down the Yukon. From the Klondike he trekked ever northward, on up to the edge of the Arctic Ocean.

A tribe of Red Indians adopted this lonely paleface gypsy as one of their own. He met few white men; but among them was a Klondike miner who had a wonderful collection of photographs of Eskimos and caribou. With the generosity of lonesome places he turned the whole works over to his friend, Thomas.

It was this sourdough's chance gift that set young Thomas up in business as a skaid, a tale-teller. He started giving illustrated talks about Alaska to audiences, and found they liked it. He entered his fourth university, Princeton, where he was both student and instructor. Surreptitiously, he made little trips away to other towns and gave his talks. They were liked still better; so with a camera again he headed for Alaska the next summer. That autumn he found he could make as much in one night's talking as he could teaching for two weeks. Why teach?

Young Thomas had a silver tongue and a way with him; *but there's no such thing as genius; he worked like a horse to do the job right.* Franklin K. Lane, then Secretary of the Interior, heard him, got him up before the Smithsonian, thought up a fine scheme for Thomas to go all around this country opening people's eyes to its wonders. The war came, and Lane decided that Thomas's trained eye and tongue could be put to still better uses. Why not send him to Europe with a roving commission to visit all fronts and report what he saw to the people of the United States? There was no appropriation for such services; but Thomas himself got eighteen anonymous gentlemen of Chicago to put up the money. E. P. Ripley, builder of the Santa Fe Railway, was one of them. Silas Strawn, president of the American Bar Association, was another. With an expert cameraman and assistants, Fate's pet child set sail.

He was in the midst of it on the Western front, with the Italian forces in the Alps on skiis, on the Asiago Plateau and along the Piave River. In Venice he heard of General Allenby's appointment to command the Allied forces in the Near East. By heavens, he thought, that will be a picturesque and dramatic campaign—Jerusalem and Mecca, haunted with age-old stories; here is meat for both me and the camera! He got in touch with the British War Office, and they obligingly sent along a vessel to take Fate's pet child over to Cairo.

There he and Harry Chase, his photographer, hopped aboard a plane and, as Thomas has said several thousand times, *made in forty minutes* a journey that had taken the *Children of Israel forty years.* He stuck with Allenby's army many months, photographing like mad, enjoying it all hugely and getting into tight places—as when he made photographs in a certain mosque in Hebron and came within an ace of being torn to bits by a mob of outraged Mahometans.

Throughout this country he kept hearing rumors of strange happenings far to the south, in the Arabian Desert, where a mysterious British officer had united the hostile Arab tribes and was helping them in a fierce holy war against the Turks. On this man's head the Turks had placed a price of a quarter of a million dollars, dead or alive. Yet he led a charmed life, and any man who harmed him would be stewed in the oil of a terrible vengeance. General Allenby finally told Thomas that this unusual person was Colonel T. E. Lawrence. "Would you like to join him?" Allenby asked. "It could be arranged."

So Fate's pet child joined Lawrence in the heart of a desert land closed to Christians for thirteen centuries. So he saw much of the desert war. So he squatted with Lawrence in a wool tent, sipping thick sweet coffee and arguing obscure matters of archaeology. So he loped over sandy miles on camel-back with Lawrence's hard-bitten Bedouins, while Lawrence rode ahead and maybe perused Aristophanes in the original, going to some rendezvous with death. So he saw Lawrence blow up Turkish railroad trains with devilish cunning and between whiles discuss Arabic poetry and keep his desert devils happy. So he wandered through the ghost street of the lost lovely city of Petra, chiseled out of the solid rock, where Lawrence won a smashing victory.

The storyteller's instinct in Thomas thrived and waxed and grew fat in those days. He knew that in this quiet Englishman at the head of his thousands of Bedouin he had the story of the ages. Lord, what a tale!

With the armistice Thomas came back to France. But there were still tight places where a storyteller could poke an adventurous nose. Germany was in revolution, but what was going on there the outside world did not know. It was forbidden to enter; and *that word forbidden was always an invitation to Thomas.* After many frustrated attempts he almost literally crawled on his belly through French barbed wire and between French sentries into Germany. There he hobnobbed with Liebknecht and Rosa Luxembourg, saw the streets of Berlin run red and got away by suavely tricking the commander of a French gunboat into taking him aboard. In Paris he was sent for by Colonel House to report on what he had seen in Germany and at last he came back to the United States.

Now Thomas, as they say, knows his onions when it comes to entertaining the public. In New York he rented a theater and put on his show, the tale of Lawrence and of Allenby. It ran for weeks; he contracted for a string of theaters across the country the following fall. On his very last night in New York Fate brought along a certain Percy Burton to see the show—one-time manager of Henry Irving and Sir Johnston Forbes-Robertson.

Mr. Burton was quite bowled over. He got in touch with Thomas at once and very persuasively asked him to take the thing over to England. All right, said Thomas, if you will get me the Royal Opera House and an invitation from the British government. Mr. Burton met both these naive requests, so Thomas bade good-bye to $30,000 he had paid on his American contracts and made for London, where he was to have a run in the British Empire longer than Frank Bacon's famous run in "Lightnin."

In the South Seas and in India he gathered more adventure material. He was leaving India when this pet child of Fate got another opportunity—a round-about invitation from the Amir of Afghanistan to visit that country, till then another of the spots hitherto forbidden to Europeans. It happened that the Amir was then coquetting for recognition.

So Thomas went through forbidden Khyber Pass, on India's north border, and into that old stamping-ground of invading hordes of Scythians, Persians, Greeks, Seljuks, Tartars, Mongols, Durani and every other tribe or people bent on pulling a plum out of India's pie. On the way he passed through Waziristan, the world's navel of bedevilment, as he calls it, where brigandage is respectable and the heat singes your eyebrows. And if you want to know how he fared in Afghanistan, read "Beyond Khyber Pass."

In 1924 the American government suddenly sent word to Fate's pet child that they wanted some one to do the history of the first world flight, and would he take it on? (The world is Thomas's oyster, and the spice for it just comes to him!) He was sorry the inspiration had not hit the government earlier—the flight was then *nearing its end;* but he joined and finished out the latter stages of the epochal journey. The thing put the finishing touch to his enthusiasm for flying; he was a competent pilot himself; he figured that now the age of wings had come and it was up to him to take mother and grandmother and the kids everywhere by air. He compromised by going with Mrs. Thomas on a 25,000-mile air journey in Europe. The product of that was "European Skyways."

His next job was the story of Count Luckner, the merry Sea Devil who played hob with Allied shipping during the war. This was a best-seller. *Thomas enjoys writing about the other fellow more than about himself, and he likes writing better than speaking,* though he confesses that getting a good audience well worked up is much like getting high on champagne. Just recently he finished the story of the German U-boats, a story for which he was collecting material for two years.

For a couple of years now Lowell Thomas has been living on a farm. I found him there recently, dressed in well-worn khaki and contemplating the cows. These are the only two peaceful years he has had; he says feelingly that he and Mrs. Thomas have been married eleven years, and during the first nine they never had a chance to unpack their wedding presents.

There is a string of interesting visitors to that farm from pretty much all over the world, many of them dropping in from the air. The house is at least a hundred years old, and Thomas works in an enviable attic big as a manor hall. He keeps fit by playing every kind and sort of athletic game. He has to keep fit; the next trip of this extraordinary couple may take them to any old corner of the earth, Central Africa or the Arctic; they may have to be at home on ski, snowshoe, dog sled, horse, donkey, camel, elephant, auto or airplane.

However, Thomas confesses to a hankering nowadays for staying right there at home. He has been bitten by an insidious desire to make that farm pay—which is a somewhat tougher job than penetrating forbidden Afghanistan. Still, he is Fate's pet child; who knows? He might succeed in doing even that.

In world-familiar "campaign" hat, with the then-dictator of Albania, Essad Pasha who was assassinated a fortnight later.

With a Burmese sultan, the Swaba of the Shan States.

With wife, Fran, relaxing in tropical Eden, an island off the Malay Peninsula.

A postponed honeymoon: L.T. and wife heading into Malay Forest.

"Forbidden" countries attracted Lowell like magnets. Here about to cross the frontier into Afghanistan, then one of the world's least-known nations.

L.T. chats with King Amanullah Khan (in black astrakhan) of then "Forbidden" Afghanistan, and several of King's brothers in the grounds of the royal palace at Kabul.

SECTION 3

The successful soldier-author-editor Francis Yeats-Brown, whose interrupted British Army career as the fourth son of a prominent English family is described by Lowell in the introduction to this book, was "an aristocrat to his finger tips."

He spoke with an Oxford accent and wore a monocle and to the part was born.

Yet underneath his British frosting, he was an enthusiastic, perceptive, discerning journalist, interested in everything about him.

Many Americans will remember him as a successful speaker, who toured the nation, incidentally starting his tour in the Assembly Hall in Salt Lake City, in the Thirties.

A long-time friend of Lowell, 'Y.B.' penned the following profile for This Week Magazine *in 1936.*

He Tells the World

By FRANCIS YEATS-BROWN *Author of "Lives of a Bengal Lancer,"*
"Golden Horn," etc. and editor of "The Spectator." (1926)

That resonant and magnetic voice of Mr. Lowell Thomas, heard nightly by expectant multitudes from the Atlantic to the Pacific oceans, is not only the most expensive in the world, but also the most expansive: it costs $1,000,000 to put on the air, and 20,000,000 people listen to it. It brings him the largest "fan mail" in the world.

His also is the face that launches a thousand newsreels. Just how many he has actually produced I don't know, but a thousand is certainly a serious understatement for he appears every day in every one of the fifteen thousand cinemas that take the Fox Movietone service. He is as popular on the screen as he is on the air, where a recent test has revealed that his talk is the first favorite among the regular features. In all history, no one person has been so long, so often and so successfully before the public.

To me, as an Englishman, such a figure would be interesting anyway, for nobody in my country could gather such a vast audience, much less hold its attention for many years without a break; and I have another reason, or excuse, for writing this article. I happened to have known "Tommy" for more than fifteen years, long before his apotheosis, so that he has an added interest to me as a kind of symbol or portent of this age. This age of miracles.

He seems to me a typical American, and by knowing him well (as I believe I do) I feel that I have met a considerable number of the citizens of the United States. Long ago, he told me that he wanted space and sport: a house in the country and horses to ride. He has them now. Reforming the world does not interest him. He has no ax to grind—or if he has, he keeps it at his country home. For the rest, he is content to watch the world roll by regarding it with a practiced eye for entertainment values. The life of cities bores him. Although the newsreels demand from him two sleepless nights a week in New York, and the radio its daily toll, his heart is in the Berkshire Hills.

He runs a local baseball team. He has an adventure library of 5,000 volumes. The other day he took me hunting rattlesnakes. When he can, he breakfasts in his riding boots. Some time ago he acquired an unmanageable outlaw horse, which he tamed and gentled on his farm so that now it is one of the best performers in his stable. I am sure that his success with that reformed runaway gives him more pleasure than any of his public achievements.

I said he had no ax to grind: that is certainly the chief reason for his popularity on the radio. People will listen to propaganda for just so long, but what they need is news and entertainment rather than views and improvement. He is a factual commentator and proud of it. He won't take sides in any issue; and he nurses no Napoleonic complex in his bosom. Behind his talk is a lifetime of experience as a journalist and raconteur and a strong and simple personality.

Sir Jagadis Bosé, the famous Indian scientist, once made a profound observation when he said to me: "All great things are simple." At the time I did not see the wisdom of this remark, but now that I have met many outstanding men (Mussolini at the beginning of Fascism; Venizelos when he held Greece in his hands; Lawrence of Arabia; scientists, financiers, politicians, even one saint) I have discovered that they are all simple. The near-great are complex. So are crooks.

Lowell Thomas' personality comes so clearly and so brilliantly over the ether because of his simplicity. He has no ulterior object, nothing to hide, no purpose but to tell us the day's big news as vividly as he can. (How arrestingly he does it is very evident to a Londoner like myself, who is condemned to listen at home to the jaded voices of our heavily censored announcers.)

"Tommy" has an infectious enthusiasm for the passing scene, and he knows too much of the world to want to change it or uplift it; rather he presents it to us as a show. His voice is friendly, virile, typically American, yet without trace of local accent; he speaks for all the United States, and is heard from Canada to the Caribbean.

No doubt his early years provided a background for his success. His boyhood was passed in a Colorado gold mining camp, 10,000 feet above sea level. I dare say his lung-power may derive from a childhood spent at these high altitudes, but I remember also that he once told me that his father, a mining surgeon, trained him from infancy in elocution. He worked his way through various colleges as janitor, salesman, night-cook; he punched cows, pitched alfalfa, was a reporter in Cripple Creek, Denver, and Chicago and a graduate student at Princeton. He knows the life of the people from A to Z. The Great War found him with a staff of cameramen on the Western Front.

One afternoon in early 1918, when he was strolling across the Square of San Marco in Venice, he saw a bulletin from Rome pinned up on a sandbag; it announced that General Allenby was about to drive the Turks from the Holy Land. Here was romance besides which the "Bride of the Adriatic" grew pale. Within an hour, he had left Italy for Palestine.

Soon he was camping on the Mount of Olives with the Cockneys who were to take Jerusalem. Those were great days, when a thousand years of prophecy found their fulfillment. He saw the occupation of Bethlehem and Jericho, battles at Jaffa and the Sea of Galilee, the taking of Tyre, Australian horsemen riding through Nazareth.

In the Holy City he met Colonel T. E. Lawrence, smoothshaven, blue-eyed, dressed as a Prince of Mecca. Lawrence was then at the height of his extraordinary career. Thomas made friends with him at once—as he does with all who share with him the love for high adventure—and left no film untaken that could record the remarkable exploits of this young hero.

When the war ended, he delighted London with the story of the shy student who had turned soldier and had led his Arabs first to Jeddah and then on to the final triumph at Damascus. "With Lawrence in Arabia" played to full houses in Covent Garden and even in the enormous Albert Hall; it was the talk of Great Britain. We English are a modest race, but we were enchanted to hear, from the lips of an American, how one of us had helped to win the Great War. A million people saw that Lowell Thomas film presentation. More millions flocked to "Tommy's" doors as he traveled round the world.

When he came to India on one of his world tours, I was attached to his party as interpreter and liaison officer. My desire was to see that he met the right people and took the right pictures from the point of view of the Indian government. However, he generally did what he wanted and saw whom he pleased. His energy was immense, and he spared no trouble or money to obtain the best pictures and information.

We went everywhere from Cape Comorin, at the southernmost tip of the Peninsula, to Afghanistan, whose Amir paraded his Court and even played polo before the motion picture camera. We interviewed agitators and saints, saw the Car of Juggernaut at Puri, and the miraculous hand of St. Francis Xavier at Goa. We were blessed by the Three-Breasted Goddess at Madura and drank tea with Afridi free-booters at Kus; it was a marvelous trip from my point of view, and I think from his, although the large sum of money (was it a quarter of a million dollars?) which he spent in making "Through Romantic India" could it yield him an adequate return?

Two years later I met Lowell Thomas in Boston. In a small way my own experiences had been somewhat similar to his for I had bought the rights of another illustrated picture ("Climbing Mount Everest") and had been trying to show it in Canadian cinemas in competition with such attractions as "The Thief of Bagdad" and "Flaming Youth." Poor Tibetan devil dancers, poor climbers plodding up a snowy slope—they could not rival the glamour of a Fairbanks or a Colleen Moore! I was broke. "Tommy" had troubles of his own, but he did his best to help me and taught me all I know (which isn't much) of the art of public speaking.

Having discovered that making personal appearances in theaters was too wearing, Lowell Thomas took to authorship, and wrote no less than twenty books in the intervals of traveling to and fro, speaking in every city in the United States with a population of more than five thousand. It was during these years that he bought his estate in Dutchess County and hitched his wagon to the rising star of radio.

Here he is now: speaker, traveler, author and adventurer at heart. Life has given him much during the last fifteen years and he has also given back much to the life of his time. He has "walked with Kings, nor lost the common touch." He has faced difficulties and come up smiling. He has won fame and wealth, and better still, a great place in the minds of the people.

With it all, he remains simple and unspoiled; a home-loving, sport-loving man.

He has made a fine art of the management of time; had he not done so, he would never get any exercise, and would soon be crushed under the weight of his correspondence. As it is, he seems never hurried, always to have leisure for his friends. Whenever he travels, and in many spare moments of the day, you may see him with a secretary and a suitcase full of letters; these are but a hundredth part of his daily mail, which is dealt with by his staff.

I suppose few busy Americans spend as much time as "Tommy" does at play. I have said that he breakfasts in his boots. Every morning, when in the country, he rides through the forest trails and over the hills of his estate. He swims. He plays tennis. He skis. He has a fur farm which interests him extremely. He is always building. He is making a jumping lane for his horses. All the family (Mrs. Lowell Thomas, Pherbia Thomas, his widely travelled sister, and eleven-year-old "Sonny") take a delight in out-of-door sports. "Sonny" has the kind of perfect seat on a horse which can be acquired only in childhood: for two years his father made him ride bareback, so that now he seems part of his mount.

I think "Tommy's" love of privacy must come from the Anglo-Saxon stock of his forebears. People used to linger on the state highway to see his country home. Now they can no longer do so, for he has diverted the state highway, and planted a barrier of trees and brush to keep his garden far from the maddening crowd. There I must leave him with his dogs; he is probably on his way to the stables or off on a cross-country ski trip.

He was the first to broadcast regularly from a studio near his home. For a "live audience" his Irish Setter "Buttons."

Nearing the end of man's first flight around the world, 1924. Top: Capt. Lowell Smith officer in command. Standing left to right: Lt. Leigh Wade, Major Corliss C. Moseley, Lt. H. H. Ogden, Lt. Les Arnold, and Lt. John Harding holding mascot "Frank" on chain. Maj. Moseley was flying L.T. at the time. Lt. Burdette Wright, then aide to Gen. Billy Mitchell, later head of Curtiss Wright Corp.

Native riflemen and camels guard three remaining planes at Karachi. Two out of four finally made it all the way around world.

At Tempelhof Aerodrome, Berlin, 1926: Mr. and Mrs. L.T. with Gustave Lindenthal, famous patriarch and builder of the great bridges across the Hudson River. In the background: Otto Merkle, founder and head of the German Airlines—Lufthansa.

Early aerial conquerors of the Atlantic, in 1931, honoring Dr. James Kimball, weather wizard. Top, left to right: Lon Yancy (first to fly to Italy), Charles Lindbergh, Frank Courtney, Armand Lotti, Harry O'Conner, and Bernt Balchen, who also piloted Byrd over the South Pole. Seated: Clarence Chamberlain, Amelia Earhart, Dr. Kimball, Ruth Elder, Peter Brady, James Fitzmaurice, and L.T. It was Dr. Kimball who told them whether and when they could take the chance.

Helping the Dionne Quintuplets celebrate a birthday at Calandar, Ontario. Mrs. Thomas assists.

Having made his first flights in 1917 in Egypt, Palestine and Arabia, here he is in 1922 with an early flier who achieved unusual success in his field. Major Henry (Hap) Arnold flew as Lowell's pilot in the early Signal Corps open biplanes and later went on to command over two million U.S. airmen in World War II. The day this picture was taken Hap and Lowell cracked up in a "Jerry."

SECTION 4

The following two sketches are by two men who differed greatly in their relationship with Lowell.

This first excerpt is from his "To Hell in a Handbasket," by humorist H. Allen Smith whose even more famous best seller "Low Man on a Totem Pole," was a popular favorite through the 1930's and 40's. He and L.T. only met at a Prohibition Era "binge" described herewith.

Dale Carnegie, on the other hand, was a longtime friend and confidente.

The Carnegie book, "How To Win Friends and Influence People" became an all-time best seller, with millions of copies printed since first published in the Thirties, and is still widely sold throughout the world.

A Literary Tea for Lowell Thomas

By H. ALLEN SMITH *Author of "Low Man on a Totem Pole," many other humorous works.*

The months I spent on Park Row coincided with the period of the literary tea. It was unthinkable that a book should be published without a party for its author on publication day, and all such parties were called literary teas. In 1930 I received my first invitation to one of these soirees and I accepted it eagerly. I sometimes felt like pinching myself to see if it were all true—me, a literary critic, and now being accepted into the cultural life of the greatest city in the world.

Jim Monahan, of the Century Company, invited me to attend a literary tea at the home of Lowell Thomas, whose latest book, *Land of the Black Pagoda,* was being published by Century. The Thomas apartment was a duplex, beautifully furnished, tastefully decorated, an altogether fitting residence for the famous explorer-author and so on who was even then beginning to branch out into radio. Mr. Thomas had never had a literary tea before, nor had he ever attended one. Jim Monahan knew about literary teas and suggested that this one be held in a hotel suite but Mr. Thomas said, "I should say not! We have this perfectly charming apartment and, after all, these are newspaper people, *my* kind of people, and I *want* them to be in my home."

By the time I got there both floors of the apartment were crowded with people. Mr. Monahan had provided an ample supply of Golden Wedding whisky and the créme de la créme of the literati were already belting it down as fast as they could. In the first hour the effects of the drinking began to show. Voices were raised. A couple of fist fights were broken up. I met a man named Harold Matson and had a couple of Golden Weddings with him while we talked about San Francisco, where he had been a newspaperman. I had a few more drinks and met Burton Rascoe, one of the most widely known literary critics of the time. He had come out of Oklahoma, spent some time in Chicago, and I had heard a lot about him.

I found him leaning against a door, his eyes half closed, a highball glass sagging in his hand. I approached him and introduced myself. He told me to go away and not bother him. Just like Will Rogers. I put on an air of terrible hurt and with a throb in my voice said: "I have looked forward to this moment for years—the achievement of my one flaming ambition—to meet the great Burton Rascoe. I am the founder and first president of the Burton Rascoe Literary Club of Tulsa. There are a hundred and eighty members and they meet every Tuesday evening and read aloud from the works of Burton Rascoe. And now . . . now . . . I meet him, and he tells me to go away. I bowed my head and sobbed. Mr. Rascoe shook himself like a wet dog and put a hand on my shoulder. "Really," he said, "I didn't know. Great heavens, I didn't even know there *was* a Burton Rascoe Club in Tulsa. Please! Please have a drink with me."

"You can go straight to hell," I said to him. "I'm sorry I ever founded the stinking club. You can just kiss my foot."

I turned and walked away. He pursued me, and continued pursuing me, during the rest of the evening. He'd come up behind me and grab me by the arm and begin apologizing again and, of course, both he and I were getting more stimulated all the whole. So I saw a pretty female standing by herself and someone told me she was Francine Larrimore, the actress, and I went up to her and tried to make like John Barrymore, and she spurned me, and so I went into the Burton Rascoe act again—I was the founder and first president of the Francine Larrimore Society, made up of people who simply worshiped the ground she walked on, and now at last my god look at how long this sentence is getting. Miss Larrimore reacted the same way Burton Rascoe had reacted, and now I had *two* important people trailing me around, trying to worm their way back into the good graces of the founder of their respective fan clubs. Harry Hansen was there for a while, and Carl Van Doren, and Lyle Saxon from New Orleans, and something over a hundred other people in varying stages of stimulation. Some of these, perhaps a fourth of all those present, were professional free-loaders, or gate-crashers. I would run into many such creatures later on—people who got most of their food supply and their drinks by walking into parties where they had not been invited. They were of two kinds—the garrulous, who could talk convincingly on almost any subject, and the strong, silent, mysterious type. They were real bums and chiselers, but they gave much thought and preparation to their profession. I think I have all the qualifications for their line of work save one: a passion for canapés.

In one room of the Thomas apartment a screen had been set up and Mr. Thomas was supposed to show films of his travels in India. There were folding chairs and a projector and Mr. Thomas did get started on his illustrated program, but he never finished it. Drunks wandered in and out of the room and fell over the chairs and stayed a few minutes and some of them heckled Mr. Thomas, yelling, "Shut up fer ——sakes!" and "Go straddle a camel!" Mr. Thomas finally gave up. I caught glimpses of him during the evening and he did not have the appearance of a happy and content host. His wife, Frances, a person of gentility, wandered from room to room, watching people slopping drinks on her furniture and on her carpets, listening to the yelling and quarreling, looking at the people sprawled indecently on the stairway, kissing and hugging one another. Some said she wrung her hands a little.

I can remember that as the hour grew late someone was making an effort to get people to leave, and occasionally there would be the sound of splintering wood—who knows how much furniture was wrecked that night. I was wandering around trying to find somebody else to insult me, so that I could organize another fan club, and I noticed that my eyes had a tendency to close, and they must have closed, for the next thing I remember it was daylight and I was in the apartment of Harold Matson, the fellow from San Francisco. He has been my literary agent for twenty-odd years (*odd* is the word) and my close friend longer than that. Because of him I count it a blessing that I accepted the invitation to my first literary tea. I went to many of them after that and they were all just as charmingly cultural as the tea for *Land of the Black Pagoda.*

Long years afterward I was talking to Lowell Thomas and I reminded him of the party. He grabbed his head in his hands and said, almost in a whisper, "Please! Please don't say another word! I have traveled all over the world, I've been through hell, I've brushed elbows with death a dozen times, but that was my hour of true horror. I'd just as soon I never heard about it again as long as I live."

al Phyfe

"Good evening, everybody" and "So long until tomorrow" were first used in 1930 on a daily program that has broken all records.

Radio listeners of the late Twenties will remember War Correspondent Floyd Gibbons, right. Lowell succeeded Floyd, in September, 1930 and has been on the air at the same hour ever since.

With the late H.V. Kaltenborn with whom he so long shared radio pioneer hours.

With famed personalities of the 1930's. Front, Major Bowes, Ed Wynn; back, Jack Pearl, Lowell Thomas, Paul Whiteman, David Warfield and James Brady.

His, also was the first television news program, and this the studio scene of historic telecast, October 19, 1943. All TV was shelved during the War. Later he concentrated on radio until film made it possible to put on his "High Adventure" TV series.

During his early years on the air, he shared the prime evening spot with the fantastically popular team of Amos 'n Andy. Top, as they appeared in 1930; then, 30 years later at the Hollywood Brown Derby, Freeman Gosden and Charles Correll.

A gold-plated microphone on his 10th anniversary, presented by NBC President, Niles Trammel.

CBS President William S. Paley presented a rare Chinese bowl to mark his 20th anniversary. Since then he has ignored anniversaries. 1967 was the 38th.

He Dictates in Taxicabs
and Travels 5000 Miles

By DALE CARNEGIE *Author of "How To Win Friends and Influence People" and other books.* (1944)

One spring day in 1916 my telephone rang and a man who was doing graduate work in constitutional law and teaching at Princeton University asked for an appointment. He wanted someone to help him in the preparation and delivery of an illustrated address on Alaska. When I met him the next day, I was immensely impressed, because that young man possessed just about everything necessary for success—an attractive personality, contagious enthusiasm, astonishing energy, and boundless ambition. I prophesied then that someday he would be both rich and famous.

Now my prophecies very often go wrong, but, for once, I was right. That man became almost an American institution. As far as riches are concerned—well, his income is a secret, of course, but *Time Magazine* once estimated that he earned about 200,000 dollars a year.

His name is Lowell Jackson Thomas, but his wife and his intimate friends call him "Tommy." Tommy has been broadcasting the news to the Eastern half of the United States five days a week, without a break, since 1930—an all-time record for a daily sponsored network program. Also, since 1934 he has been giving the news to the nation every week through the Fox Movietone Newsreel.

During those years of broadcasting, Lowell Thomas has said "So long until tomorrow" thousands of times, and has spoken millions of words—enough to fill nearly a hundred books.

When I first met Lowell Thomas, he was giving travel talks on Alaska for a few dollars a night, as a sideline to his work at Princeton. I have watched him climb from those days of obscurity up to the top of the ladder. Yet he is still the same modest, sincere, unaffected, considerate man today that he was when I first knew him. In all those years I have never heard anyone criticize Lowell Thomas for anything. If he has even one enemy in this world, I don't know who it is.

Reprinted with permission from Dorothy Carnegie.

Lowell Thomas' life was deeply influenced by his mother and his father. Both had been teachers, but his father finally gave up teaching for medicine. His father, by the way, although in his seventies, is still practicing medicine in Asbury Park, New Jersey, and recently been handling the medical and surgical problems for an immense naval project.

When Tommy was a boy, his imagination was fired by the travel and adventure stories of Marco Polo, Magellan, Daniel Boone, and Robinson Crusoe. He resolved then that someday he, too, would travel to the far corners of the earth and would set his adventures down in books. Few men have ever been so successful as Lowell Thomas in transferring their dream castles into the stern stuff of reality.

He spent years roaming over Europe, Asia, Alaska, and Australia. He toured India with the Prince of Wales and was the first American traveler ever officially invited to enter and photograph the wild country of Afghanistan. The Governments of India and Burma and the Federated Malay States gave him special trains and river boats and placed strings of elephants at his command, so that he could explore and photograph their strange sights and customs.

He has written over forty books whose very titles ring with the spirit of adventure—books with titles such as *With Lawrence in Arabia, Beyond Khyber Pass, Pageant of Adventure,* and *These Men Shall Never Die.*

Even as a boy, Lowell Thomas dreamed not only of traveling, but also of telling about his travels. He knew that in order to accomplish that ambition, he would have to get an education. He went in for schooling on a large scale, acquiring four college degrees from four educational institutions: Valparaiso University, the University of Denver, Kent College of Law in Chicago, and Princeton University.

He didn't have the money to attend one university, let alone four. During his summer vacations he punched cattle and pitched alfalfa on the Ute Indian Reservation. He worked as a gold miner in Cripple Creek, Colorado. Later he worked as a reporter on Denver and Chicago newspapers.

He paid for his board and room during the winter by caring for furnaces and acting as a waiter and as a short-order cook in a restaurant. He fed and milked a cow for one of his professors. He sold real estate. He did a bit of teaching and lecturing on the side. Back in 1915 the first World War stopped all tourist travel to Europe. That gave Lowell Thomas an idea: why not prepare illustrated talks on the scenic wonders of America? It was a good idea, but it required cash for railroad fares, hotels, photography. Lowell Thomas had no money, but he did have a contagious enthusiasm that has made him one of the best salesmen in America. He persuaded railroad and steamship companies to send him on a deluxe tour, with all expenses paid, throughout the West and up into Alaska. I heard Tommy's address on Alaska; it was full of sweep and gusto and his pictures were superb.

Franklin K. Lane, Secretary of the Interior in President Wilson's Cabinet, also heard that speech. He was instantly captivated. When America declared war on Germany in 1917, Lane persuaded President Wilson to send Lowell Thomas abroad to take pictures of the war and then to return with a series of illustrated productions that would arouse the fighting spirit of the folks back home.

There was only one catch to the appointment, but it was a serious one: the job carried no salary and no expense money.

Lowell Thomas induced a group of eighteen millionaires in Chicago to lend him 100,000 dollars to finance his trip abroad to take pictures of the first World War. Eighteen months later he returned to the United States with colored and motion pictures of the fighting, not only in France, Belgium, Italy, and the Balkans, but also of General Allenby's picturesque campaign in the Holy Land—a campaign that swept the Turks out of Jerusalem, Jericho, Bethlehem, and Nazareth, and knocked Turkey out of the war. What was even more sensational, he brought back the story of the most picturesque and romantic figure produced by the first World War—Lawrence of Arabia, the young, shy, silent archeologist who organized the sheiks of the Arabian desert into a guerrilla force which dynamited Turkish railroads and lines of communication.

Lowell Thomas' illustrated talks were presented at the largest theater in New York City for months. Later he was invited to London, where he, an American, told the British people the story of their own astonishing campaign in the Near East.

I had the privilege of being associated with Lowell Thomas at the time, in a business way. I saw London crowds stand in line for hours to buy tickets to hear him. That happened night after night, month after month. He appeared in the Covent Garden Opera House where the demand for seats was so great that the Grand Opera season of London was put off for a month so that Tommy could continue his season. Then he moved to Royal Albert Hall, where he addressed from fifteen to twenty-five thousand people every day. The British had never even heard of Lawrence of Arabia until Lowell Thomas told them his thrilling story.

For years Tommy continued giving these illustrated talks all over the world. He spoke to four million people, face to face, in more than four thousand audiences in every English speaking country on the globe.

Then in 1930 Lowell Thomas got the biggest break of his life: an opportunity to broadcast the day's news, daily, for the *Literary Digest*. That was what started him toward his position of prominence in the world of affairs. Tommy gave ten broadcasts each week, and then stayed up all night, two nights a week, doing the Fox Movietone Newsreel. He also answered a vast amount of mail and turned out a book or two each season.

How could he possibly do it all? The answer is that he built a capable organization around himself; and, in addition, Tommy knew how to make every minute count. I was with him one time in London when he was leaving for Australia. He not only dictated letters to his secretary in the taxicab as we were driving to the ship, but he stood on the dock, dictating across a fence. He was still dictating letters two minutes before the gangplank was hauled up.

Lowell Thomas doesn't give a hoot for night clubs, parties, or society. His hobbies are horseback riding, softball, and skiing. Skiing isn't a hobby with him—it's an obsession. During the winters he sometimes travels five thousand miles for one week of skiing.

Lowell Thomas married Frances Ryan, a girl of exquisite charm whom he met at the University of Denver. They have one son, Lowell Thomas, Junior, who is already a world traveler and an explorer. He is also a ski expert who has outstripped his dad.

Lowell Thomas one evening found himself in front of the microphone with five pages of his news broadcast missing. That meant his broadcast was about five minutes short, and the time had to be filled in by a studio musician. The catastrophe had been caused by the oversight of a secretary. But Lowell Thomas didn't scold her. When she began to apologize, he told her to forget it. He assured her that the batting average was excellent and that nothing else counted. Tommy never raises his voice or loses his temper. He is an expert in the fine art of human relations.

One day, many years ago, while he was giving a series of illustrated lectures in Boston, a group of angry creditors swooped down on him at the end of a performance. At that period of his career he was not only dead broke, but he faced pressing obligations that he couldn't possibly discharge at once. It's true he had made a fortune. He had grossed a million dollars in one year while still in his twenties. *But through a series of unfortunate reverses, he had also lost a fortune.* These creditors and their attorneys were determined to take possession of his camera, films, and projection equipment. Thomas received them as though they had been honored guests, served them tea in his dressing room, sympathized with them, and then pointed out in his sincere, gracious manner that his only hope of paying them soon was to continue what he was doing. The creditors had arrived irritated and angry. They left feeling that they were personal friends of Lowell Thomas. But here is the real point of the story: he later paid them every single cent he owed them! That's "Tommy" for you.

"I realize you are capable of twisting your tongue to pronounce all nationalities."

"Lowell Thomas tells all the bad news."

His career has sparked many cartoons over the decades. Here are some of Otto Soglow's impressions, Soglow of Little King fame.

HERBERT HOOVER

The Waldorf Astoria Towers
New York, New York
September 10, 1959

My dear Lowell:

Your speech on the occasion of the
great honor extended to me by the Mayor
and the City of New York still echoes in my
mind.

If I have to have a reincarnation I
would prefer it to be Lowell Thomas above
all others. It would be an eternal life of
adventure, of courage and of public service.

I can only add that I am grateful for
all these years of your friendship.

Yours faithfully,

Herbert H.

Mr. Lowell Thomas
Hammersley Hill
Pawling, New York

Gonzalez Studio

Former President Herbert Hoover at Clover Brook Farm, Quaker Hill, near Pawling, New
York, "President Hoover wrote his first post-White House speech at our home," and then
his host added, "He was the wisest man I ever knew, with a vast knowledge and under-
standing of the world, its inhabitants, and its problems. From the Twenties to his death
in 1964, he counted L.T. a close friend whom he often visited.

A highlight each year was an annual ball game in which FDR's "The Roosevelt Packers" played Lowell's "Nine Old Men." Picture taken in 1938, year of the Supreme Court controversy. (Further details in Sports section.)

King George of Greece, father of the present King Constantine. He it was who led Greece through World War I and the post-war period.

Interviewing pre-World War II Philippine leader, President Osmeno in Manila, accompanied by Major Chester Ray of MacArthur's staff.

With the colorful General George Patton at his headquarters in Germany the day he put on his fourth star.

With famed World War I ace, Eddie Rickenbacker, and World War II Shangri-La bomber of Japan, Gen. Jimmy Doolittle.

SECTION 5

The byline of Eleanor Harris has long been familiar to magazine readers, especially to those who follow the Reader's Digest (in which the following article appeared in 1948).

In private life, she is the wife of Jack Howard, head of the great Scripps-Howard chain of newspapers.

The Stranger Everyone Knows

By ELEANOR HARRIS *Author and writer whose works have appeared in major magazines.*

A storm was drenching night-time Denver as a man climbed into a taxicab and gave directions. Without turning around the driver said, "I'd know that voice anywhere—you're Lowell Thomas."

All over the world millions of people could say the same. The fluid, pleasant and warmly varied voice of Lowell Thomas has been broadcasting the news five days a week at exactly the same hour since 1930—the longest continuous record of any personality in radio. During those 18 years Thomas has been king of the newscasters in popularity, with rivals popping up only temporarily to dispute him. For 15 years he has also been narrating all Fox Movietone Newsreels, as well as hundreds of travelogues and short-subject films. Before his radio career he was eminently successful on the platform. From his various activities he has earned a fortune approaching ten million dollars.

Thomas's warm radio personality bears no resemblance to his appearance. He looks like a natty toy soldier grown to life-size. He is 56, with a 5 foot ten muscular body, a head of thick brown hair, and china-blue eyes set in an almost expressionless face. Absentmindedly, he sometimes shaves off half his mustache; it takes three days to grow back again. When he smiles, only the lower part of his face shifts. He seldom smokes and rarely takes a drink. One man remarked after meeting him, "A chip off the old glacier."

Nothing could be further from the truth. Behind that façade is a boiling cauldron of boyish, wild-eyed plans—to say nothing of kind deeds. Recently his secretary-shadow, Electra Ward, became engaged to his radio engineer, Gene Nicks. Thomas presented the couple with thirty acres of land; and when he learned that CBS couldn't spare the bridegroom for a honeymoon he announced, "Let's all go to the Adirondacks." So the newlyweds went on their honeymoon with Mr. and Mrs. Thomas and all the equipment necessary for getting out the nightly broadcasts.

One of Thomas's accomplishments is to run at top speed with complete dignity—which he does before every broadcast, since he is always late. On the days when he broadcasts from New York, people always enjoy watching him arrive at the CBS Building. Followed by his panting secretary, he invariably pounds up the street at a dead run. He skids into the building, jumps in and out of the elevator, gallops down the hall to the studio—and comes to a dead stop on the threshold. There he clears his throat, adjusts his tie, and strolls calmly up to his microphone. A second later he's on the air.

Thomas is paid a half-million dollars a year for his radio work, $90,000 of which he spends running what amounts to a Lowell Thomas factory. One branch is in Rockefeller Center, New York City. Here he has a seven-room suite of offices, two teletype machines, and an assorted group of employes who have worked for him for years. Like most radio newsmen, he makes no attempt to write all his scripts. Prosper Buranelli, who has been with Thomas 22 years, works with him on these as well as the newsreel narrations and books. Recently Thomas arranged for Buranelli to receive an honorary college degree originally planned for himself. "The man who cooperates with me on so much of my writing deserves this," he said. When Prosper declined to put in an appearance his pal sent an understudy to accept it for him.

Thomas prefers to work at the other branch of his factory—a fabulous estate at Quaker Hill near Pawling, N.Y., two hours from New York City. Here he has 3000 acres, a ski lift and chalet, a 90-acre lake, a softball field and bleachers, a corral for horse shows—and a mammoth red-brick mansion surrounded by 30 or 40 acres of mowed lawn. In a wing of the garage is a completely equipped broadcasting studio, with offices for two secretaries and a sound engineer.

Lowell Thomas started out toward all this munificence from Woodington, Ohio, where he was born, the only son of Harriet and Dr. Harry Thomas. His versatile doctor-father had a powerful influence on young Lowell. "He forced all his swarming hobbies on me," says Thomas. "I studied astronomy through a home telescope. At ten I knew something about comparative religions. I learned zoology, botany, geology, and especially public speaking, which my father thought everyone should know. By the time I was 14 I had made more speeches than a Presidential candidate—to audiences of

Elks and Eagles, Masons and miners."

From the time he was 21 he taught public speaking, in four colleges, and while studying for the law. On the side he also worked on local newspapers. He was juggling these occupations while teaching at Kent College in Chicago in 1915 when a friend happened to say, "Tommy, you're 23—about time you got married. Ever met a girl you'd like to have for a wife?"

Thomas thought for a long minute, then said, "Yes. A girl I used to know around the University of Denver, although I never went out with her. Her name's Frances Ryan." Another pause. "Guess I'll go to Denver and propose to her."

Thomas had no money. Then he thought of San Francisco and its coming World's fair. He went to two railroad companies in Chicago, suggested that one give him a free ride to California and the other a free ride back. In return he would write a series of newspaper articles on the beauties of the trip and the wisdom of attending the fair. Both railroads agreed. Then Thomas made arrangements with a string of papers to print the articles.

In a few days he was off. He stopped in Denver, looked up pretty Frances Ryan, and to her astonishment proposed marriage. She turned him down cold. "You've never asked me for a date, and besides I think you're stuck-up," she said—among other things.

Thomas went on to California, writing newspaper articles with one hand and letters to Miss Ryan with the other. Once west, he realized that Alaska lay nearby. He had spent his boyhood listening to miners talk about the Klondike and Nome, and quickly set about arranging a free trip to Alaska, where he spent the summer talking to Alaskans and taking motion pictures. Then he headed for New York with an illustrated lecture.

Thomas was doing graduate work in constitutional law at Princeton and doing more than all right with his Alaska talks in 1917 when the war broke out. With the backing of three members of President Wilson's cabinet he worked out a plan that involved Government influence and a group of Chicago millionaires' money— a tour of the Allied war fronts to collect material and movies that would explain to America what the war meant to Europe. Soon he had $75,000 at his disposal, a veteran photographer named Harry Chase and potent letters of introduction to all Allied commanders. He rushed to Denver and proposed to Miss Ryan again. Lowell and

Frances Thomas set out for Europe together.

After photographing the war fronts with the French, British, Belgian and American armies, Thomas decided to cover the little-known battles in the Near East. He went to Palestine and joined Allenby's cavalry. One day in Jerusalem he met the then unknown young Englishman, T. E. Lawrence, who in flowing Arabian robes was helping lead the Arabs in their drive to oust the Turks. With "the only camera in Arabia," Thomas and Chase campaigned with Lawrence. "It turned out I was the only reporter to get the story of Lawrence," Thomas recalls, "because the others didn't realize the high drama of that campaign."

Back in postwar America, Thomas hired a press agent, took huge space in the newspapers to advertise a "show" (he never referred to his performance as a "lecture" or "talk") entitled "With Lawrence in Arabia and Allenby in Palestine." He proceeded to pack the enormous Century Theater in New York City for a long run.

The English impresario Percy Burton, who had managed Forbes-Robertson, Beerbahm-Tree, Dusé and others, booked him into the famous Covent Garden Opera House and then Royal Albert Hall in London. The King and Queen came. So did the Cabinet and members of both houses of Parliament. So did Premier Clemenceau of France, the King of Spain and many others—a total of a million people in six months. The Lawrence show he eventually gave in almost every English-speaking country in the world.

When Thomas wrote the book *With Lawrence in Arabia*, his fame was further enhanced. It was a smash hit and is still bringing in royalties.

Accompanied by Mrs. Thomas, he spent the years between 1918 and 1928 traveling around the world, speaking and writing adventure books. Between trips, in 1925, the Thomases decided to find a permanent home. After a six-month search, they were driving one day on Quaker Hill, in Dutchess County, New York. As they passed a white house Thomas said, "There's the house I'd like to live in—beginning now." He rang the bell and spoke rapidly to the elderly woman who opened the door. After five minutes of Thomas talk, she invited the Thomases to move in for several months to see how they liked the house. They did, and decided to buy it.

But how? Thomas had insufficient funds. A friend suggested, "Why don't you see Doubleday, Page and get them to advance you money on a new book?"

Thomas called up Russell Doubleday and asked for a meeting with the board of directors. In front of this gathering he hastily outlined six books, verbally. Doubleday, Page gratefully presented him with the biggest advance ever given an author, and Thomas bought his house.

He then faced a tough problem: How could he write six books at once and also go on a scheduled country-wide speaking tour? The answer to this was Prosper Buranelli, then a feature writer for The New York World. Together they turned out *Count Luckner, The Sea Devil*, an instant best-seller—then proceeded on, over the years, to 38 other books, most of them adventure-biographies.

In 1930 came Thomas's biggest bonanza, the chance to broadcast news on the radio. The only full-time radio newsman in the world with a daily program, Floyd Gibbons, was about to be dropped by his sponsor, *The Literary Digest*, and they were searching for a replacement. Finally someone remembered, "Once I heard a great world war show, in London, by an American named Thomas. . . ."

Thomas was telephoned to rush to New York for an audition. CBS President Bill Paley and Thomas rounded up a committee of talented men including Ogden Nash, Dale Carnegie and Prosper Buranelli to help throw together the first news-broadcast any of them had ever heard. Thomas was signed on the spot, and for a long time was the only daily newscaster on the air. He gave the first news-broadcasts from an airplane, a submarine, a ship and a helicopter.

As an experiment during the early '30's, Western Union asked Thomas to broadcast from one of its offices, telling every listener to send him a collect telegram—for which Western Union would pay. "We'll see how many people listen to radio," said the W. U. executives expansively. Within three hours Thomas received 262,490 telegrams and Western Union had to pay for several thousand others sent collect over Postal Telegraph, its archenemy. Incidentally, this is still the all-time high in radio response.

Meanwhile, Thomas had carried out another boldly original move. A year after he had entered radio, he built his own broadcasting studio in the back yard of his home at Quaker Hill. "Why not?" he reasoned. "I can tell the news just as well from alongside my barn as from the city studio." Today, dozens of home broadcasting studios, patterned after Thomas's, stud the countryside of America.

Thomas had already completely remodeled his house, erected a gymnasium and little theater, and started a fur farm that bred mink, fox and even bear. Then one morning his wife caught him studying a hill on one side of their house. "Wouldn't that hill look much better on the other side of the house?" he asked thoughtfully.

"Now, Tommy! You can't move a hill!" objected his wife.

Two thousand truckloads of dirt later, he proved she was wrong.

After 23 years on Quaker Hill, Thomas has moved almost everything, including a whole community of friends. When he arrived, there were less than 50 other residents. Now 350 Thomas friends and acquaintances live there. He has moved his family out of the house with the movable hill into a beautiful Georgian home a few miles away. "It's fireproof," was his main argument.

In the days when Thomas E. Dewey was District Attorney of New York City, he and his wife were spending Sunday with friends in Connecticut while they pondered buying a home there. Suddenly the telephone rang for Dewey.

"This is Lowell Thomas. . . . I understand you're thinking of living in Connecticut. I have just two questions to ask you. One, have you ever seen Quaker Hill? Two, does your political future lie in Connecticut?"

"I'll be right over," said Dewey. Soon after, he and his wife arrived on Quaker Hill and were caught in the Thomas web. The price of the house Dewey liked was prohibitive for the salary of a public servant, so Thomas argued the owner into letting the Deweys live there for almost nothing to see how they liked the place. The next summer the same thing happened, and by now Dewey had worked out plans for the dairy farm which was to keep the estate self-supporting and pay for its purchase. Ever since, the Deweys have been happy residents of Quaker Hill—and warm friends of the Thomases.

Thomas has build house after house on Quaker Hill and sold them to friends, and a country club that he gave to the community. Adjoining the golf links is a clubhouse unlike any other in America. Its overwhelming fireplace tells in fragments of stone the history of mankind through the ages—a piece of the great Cheops Pyramid, a marble fragment from ancient Carthage, a part of the Taj Mahal, a slab from Rockefeller Center. And on the mantel is written in Sanskrit: "He who allows a day to pass without practicing generosity or enjoying life's pleasure is like a blacksmith's bellows—he breathes but does not live." Officially this building is called the Community Center; unofficially it is "The Barn." In it every Saturday night gathers most of Quaker Hill for a dance, with no smoking or drinking allowed.

Lowell and Fran Thomas have an army of friends and are never happier than when their house is packed with them. The place is particularly busy when Thomas's famous softball team, the Nine Old Men, is in action. This team was organized as a joke in 1932, during a friendly argument with a neighbor who lived 30 miles away, Franklin D. Roosevelt. It has boasted such players as baseball king Babe Ruth, movie actor Bob Montgomery, General Jimmy Doolittle Winthrop Rockefeller, Gene Tunney, Monroe Leaf, Lew Lehr, Dale Carnegie, Gene Sarazen, singers James Melton and Lanny Ross.

Meanwhile, Thomas seems to have acquired absolutely no feeling of self-importance. Time and again he has been the honored guest of some awe-struck small-town club, only to be sincerely awed himself by the farmer on his right, who may have thought up some new scheme for crop rotation. His house exhibits only a few mementos of his world trips and many triumphs. "My wife doesn't like the house to look like a museum," he explains, leading curious guests up to the attic where his treasures are piled haphazardly.

Thomas is now looking off serenely toward a tumultuous horizon. "I'm planning a ski tour all over the United States this year, and the publication of the ten-volume history of man, which will be told in 350 biographies from Cheops to Churchill. Then I've got a lot of future plans, too. But since the residents of Quaker Hill usually live to be a hundred, I figure I have plenty of time." He probably has, and he'll probably accomplish all his projects. Hasn't he always?

At Tokyo headquarters with Gen. MacArthur, in 1949, en route to Tibet.

With Generalissimo Chiang Kai-Shek and General Albert C. Wedemeyer on the right, at Chungking, during World War II.

Gonzalez Stud

Ike the president renews ties with L.T. who knew him as commander-in-chief of the mightiest military force in all history.

Getting some important advice from Secretary of Defense, Neil McElroy.

The Shah of Shahs and Lowell talk things over at the palace at Teheran.

A Monarch who has lived dangerously, King Hussein of Jordan.

To my very good Lowell Thoma very best wis

With Prime Minister Jawaharlal Nehru who led India through so many difficult years.

SECTION 6

Neither Maurice Zolotov, nor his subject need a lengthy introduction to most readers.

The founder and first president of the Society of Magazine Writers, Mr. Zolotov has written countless articles and books. He leans towards the fields of drama and show business and for some years was a drama critic.

Among his book subjects have been Marilyn Monroe and Alfred Lunt and Lynn Fontanne.

His Lowell Thomas profile appeared in Coronet Magazine in 1949.

The 2,000,000 Words of Lowell Thomas

By MAURICE ZOLOTOV *Drama critic and author, including books about Marilyn Monroe, Lunt and Fontanne.* (1949)

On the eighth floor of a Rockefeller Center building in New York, there exists one of the most remarkable word factories of our time. The machinery comprises two teletype machines, one teleprinter and seven typewriters. The syllable manufacturers are Lowell Thomas, two script writers and three secretaries.

Between them, this team produces some 2,000,000 words every year, a good deal of the output being composed for the Lowell Thomas' radio news program. Over the Columbia Broadcasting System, he delivers two commentaries a night, five days a week. He speaks at 6:45 to the East and Midwest, and does another broadcast at 11 P.M. with a fresh script, beamed to hit the West Coast at 8. For this, he is paid $10,000 a week by Proctor & Gamble, the soap manufacturers.

Thomas, a man of brisk friendliness, precise enunication and stentorian resonance, is probably paid more for spieling about current events than anybody in history. Besides his radio dissertations, he does the verbal obbligato for the Fox Movietone Newsreel, which has two editions a week, for which receives $1,500.

He also composes about ten articles a year for adventure magazines; turns out at least one book a year on such topics as *How to Keep Mentally Fit, Pageant of Romance* and *Stand Fast for Freedom;* and makes some twenty personal appearances during the season at $2,000 each.

Not content with all these activities, Lowell Thomas and his henchmen during 1947-48 completed a 900,000-word *Story of Mankind,* a history of the world told through the biographies of its 320 most significant men. For this, Thomas has already received a $35,000 advance from the P. F. Collier Publishing Company. Thomas has long since exceeded even such a prodigious word-smith as novelist Alexander Dumas, who turned out dozens of books with the assistance of a corps of ghost writers.

Thomas has spoken over the air for so long that he has become a fixture, like a radio tube. Yet he relishes a sort of institutional obscurity. Since 1936, he has refused to give interviews, has shunned publicity. All in all, his continuing popularity baffles students of what is known as the radio game.

Thomas neither views with alarm like Winchell nor views with gaiety like Heatter. He doesn't offer social messages or uplift. He isn't profound or ponderous. He never gives the impression that he has inside information, like Drew Pearson. Yet his rating as a newscaster has consistently been either first, second or third over the years.

"Tommy," says one of his associates, "is a guy who makes the listener feel that he doesn't know more than the listener. You figure he's a regular fellow, just like yourself—with the one advantage that he happens to be near a news wire."

Now 56, Thomas is a trim, energetic man who carries on the active athletic program of a youth of 25. He is five feet ten inches tall and weighs 165 pounds. He has small, shrewd blue eyes, set in a lean, bony face. He has a small moustache and an amiable smile, and is constantly on the move.

During the year, he probably delivers no more than 50 talks from the CBS studios in New York. Usually he gets the rough scripts from his Rockefeller Center office, either at his home in Quaker Hill, New York, or at a skiing resort. Thomas is one of the most fanatical skiers in the country, although he did not take up the sport until he was 42. From December until May, he rarely gets out of his ski boots except when he goes to bed.

At home, he skis six hours a day when the snow is right. He also travels constantly, in response to bulletins that the snow is packed just right—in Canada, Vermont or New Hampshire. Continually he is organizing ski expeditions for parties of friends or lecturing to raise money for the National Ski Patrol System, a volunteer group that rescues persons who fracture bones while skiing.

In between times, Thomas acts as a sort of tribal chieftain to a settlement of some 300 persons on Quaker Hill, an oblong plateau on the New York-Connecticut border which boasts lakes and trout streams and rolling hills.

His fervent love for this rural paradise led him into promoting Quaker Hill as the ideal spot for New York City cliff dwellers. As with skiing, he felt that all his friends and acquaintances must share the glories of the Hill. So, in order to rescue the primeval forest from the hands of real-estate developers, Thomas, in 1936, bought 3,000 acres from the Fred F. French estate. From then till now, Thomas has poured some $500,000 into making Quaker Hill one of America's unique communities.

He has built new houses. He has redecorated old houses. He has spent $45,000 on an 18-hole golf course and $5,000 having sand carted in to make a lake beach for children. He has cleared hundreds of miles of horseback trails, put up a baseball diamond and a ski tow. Residents include political leaders, judges, advertising executives, bankers, writers and publishers.

Near the highest point of Quaker Hill, Thomas has built a Community House, where Saturday-night dances or parties are staged— followed by entertainment or a brief talk given by one of Thomas' friends. Among those who have spoken or entertained are Herbert Hoover, James Melton, Robert Montgomery, Geraldine Farrar, Lanny Ross, Walter Lippman, General Eisenhower, senators, diplomats, explorers, airmen and authors galore.

The most interesting Community House item is the giant fireplace, composed of stones with historical or anthropological interest. The stones, measuring 25 feet from floor to ceiling are called "The Monuments of Man." On the lowest level are prehistoric relics. Then there are pieces from the Wailing Wall, the Washington Monument, Hitler's Reichschancellory, the English House of Parliament, the Sphinx, the North and South Poles.

Ripley sent him a Mayan image. The late Al Smith brought a slab of marble from the Empire State Building and personally cemented it. Henry Kaiser, who built the Grand Coulee Dam, contributed a sample of the dam and officiated at the stone-laying ceremonies. Nelson Rockefeller supplied a piece of Rockefeller Center. One of the rarest is a piece of the Taj Mahal, a gift of former Ambassador William Pawley.

When Thomas moved to Quaker Hill in 1926, most of the old Quaker Families had drifted away, and much of the land was not being cultivated. He stirred the Hill out of its somnolence, and trebled its population. Today, Thomas pays a formal call on every new resident, and if he discovers the new family isn't taking advantage of the recreational facilities of the Hill, he becomes disturbed.

His first extracurricular project at Quaker Hill was The Nine Old Men, a now-celebrated team of softball players that has included such worthies as Eddie Rickenbacker, Jimmie Doolittle, Gene Tunney, Colonel Stoopnagle and James Melton. The idea took shape in the sultry August of 1933, when President Roosevelt was summering at Hyde Park, together with his Brain Trust and several hundred newspaper correspondents. Thomas invited the crowd over to the Hill to cool off. About 100 showed up, and soon a softball game was under way.

From then on, the teams competed regularly. For a time, the Quaker Hill team had no name, but when Roosevelt tried to enlarge the Supreme Court, Thomas named his group The Nine Old Men. When the White House took the field next week, they wore shirts emblazoned The Roosevelt Packers.

Thomas lives at the north end of the Hill in a 32 room Georgian mansion. Over the years, he has dabbled in various kinds of farming, and lost one of his many shirts in a large dairy establishment. Likewise, he has tried raising fur-bearing animals, and currently has about 1,000 mink and foxes under cultivation. Thomas also likes to invest in unusual industrial projects.

"Just come to Tommy with plans for a helicopter factory, or oil wells, or gold mines, and he's a sucker for it," says an associate. "As for a ski-lift, he'll put money into one, any time, any place."

Thomas, who is instinctively gregarious, loves people—all kinds of people. Although his immediate family consists of his wife and a son, he usually manages to fill his mansion with guests. The scope of his friendships is remarkable. He knows literally thousands of men and women, ranging from obscure Arctic explorers and Afghan chieftains to political leaders like Churchill and de Gaulle.

Aside from his effervescent personality and knack of narrating a good story, the secret of Thomas' friendships is that he is probably the least-opinionated person alive, something hard to believe is a radio commentator. He seldom intrudes his viewpoints into a discussion. As one friend says:

"If you showed Tommy a glass of milk and asked him if it was black or white, he'd probably tell you an anecdote about Pasteur."

Although presumably an expert on issues of the day, Thomas steadfastly refuses to be a political pundit. He never analyzes the "news behind the news" for friends.

It is probably this noncommittal quality, which he carries over
into his broadcasts, that makes Thomas so consistently popular in an
age of thundering opinion-peddlers. Prosper Buranelli, his colleague
for 20 years, says: "He has few absolute opinions, and his only enemies are rattlesnakes, cannibals, Fascists and Communists." But even
these he will rarely condemn outright.

Around 1:30 each day, Thomas calls his New York word factory
and discusses the day's news with Buranelli. They rough an outline
of the 6:45 broadcast and, during the afternoon, while Thomas is
out on skis or on the golf course, his amanuenses get busy.

Each broadcast is broken down into seven or eight events. Later
in the afternoon, the segments are filed via teleprinter to Thomas'
studio and office. His secretary then retypes the items and Thomas
goes over them with a blue pencil, reshaping the words into his
colloquial vernacular.

At about 6:44—still attired in ski outfit—he strides to his private
microphone and is piped into the network at the right moment. The
cueing in and out of New York is integrated so smoothly that no
listener realizes that the announcer is 100 miles away when he feeds
Thomas the cue for his familiar sign-off, "So long until tomorrow."

The resonance of Thomas' voice, its depth and color and variety,
are the envy of public speakers and even opera singers, who invariably are amazed when they learn that Thomas' only coaching was
received from his father, a mine doctor in Cripple Creek, Colorado.

The parent, a fanatic on oratory, began to cultivate his son's
voice and diction when Tommy was two years old. By the time he
was ten, he could hold high-school audiences spellbound with
speeches on "Teddy Roosevelt and the Rough Riders" or "Should
Capital Punishment Be Abolished?"

At 18, he entered Valparaiso University in Indiana, then moved
on to the University of Denver for his M.A. In his spare time he was
a reporter on Denver papers. Next he studied at Chicago-Kent College of Law, where his skill at public speaking so hypnotized the
dean that he was put in charge of all classes in forensics. During the
summers, he made trips to Alaska to earn extra money with travel
films.

In 1915, he turned up at Princeton to study constitutional law
and annex a Ph.D. President John Grier Hibben invited him to join
the faculty. A year later, Secretary of the Interior Franklin K. Lane

decided to launch a "See America First" campaign, since World War I had shut off travel to Europe. Somebody told Lane that Professor Thomas of Princeton was an expert on Alaska. Lane was startled to find that "Professor Thomas" was a clean-shaven youth with a self-assured air.

The scholarly speakers on the program bored the audience with long, rambling speeches read from manuscripts. Then Thomas flashed his films on the screen and rattled off his Alaska speech—in swashbuckling, anecdotal style. The audience applauded for five minutes.

When America went to war, Lane remembered the Alaskan lecture and gave Thomas the assignment of compiling a cinematic history of America's fighting men. Thomas, with assistants, visited every fighting front, and even went through the lines to cover the German revolution of 1918.

Learning about General Allenby's campaign to recover Palestine from the Turks, Thomas hastened to the Holy Land with Harry Chase and covered the battles that led up to the taking of Jerusalem. Then came the great adventure of his life—his meeting with the Oxford scholar, T. E. Lawrence, who helped inspire the revolt of Arabian tribesmen against the Turkish and German armies.

Thomas broke down Lawrence's wall of reticence and got the whole dramatic story of an archaeologist who had turned guerrilla leader and won the Arabs' confidence.

Tommy returned to New York in 1919, determined not to resume his academic career. In April he rented the Century Theater and announced a series of five productions on every phase of the war. Of all his war epics, only two—"With Allenby in Palestine" and "With Lawrence in Arabia"—drew capacity audiences, so after the second week these were the only two that he presented.

Competing with top Broadway attractions, Thomas managed to fill the Century every night for three weeks. Then he took Madison Square Garden for six weeks and packed them in there. In the next ten years, he delivered his Lawrence of Arabia lecture—the same lecture with the same films—to audiences all over the world.

Meanwhile, in 1923, he had published *With Lawrence in Arabia*, which went into 30 editions, selling some 500,000 copies. Also at various times during these years, he went tiger hunting in India with the Prince of Wales, explored Afghanistan, traveled through the wilds of Australia and the Himalayan fastnesses of Upper Burma.

Then, in September, 1930, *The Literary Digest* offered to sponsor him on a five-a-week broadcast over CBS. Historically speaking, the first network commentator was H. V. Kaltenborn, in 1923, but only twice a week. Floyd Gibbons, whose machine-gun delivery brought him fame, had the first daily program. But in those early days of broadcasting, when reception was poor, Thomas' stentorian diction came through more intelligibly, assuring him a permanent place in radio. In 1932, Thomas switched over to NBC for 15 years.

On his first broadcast, Thomas set the pattern of his approach to current events. Besides Buranelli, his scripters for that day included Ogden Nash, Dale Carnegie and five volunteers. Thomas uttered these prophetic words:

"Adolf Hitler, the German Fascist chief, is snorting fire. There are now two Mussolinis in the world, which seems to promise a rousing time. Adolf is one. He has written a book called the German Fascist Bible. In it, this belligerent gentleman states that a cardinal policy of his now-powerful German party is the conquest of Russia. That's a tall assignment, Adolf. You just ask Napoleon!"

Since then, a lot of words have flowed through his microphone and a lot of world-shaking history has been made, but through it all Lowell Thomas has managed to maintain equanimity. During the rousing New Deal years, so impartial was Thomas' approach to Roosevelt that listeners did not suspect that Thomas leaned to the Republican Party, or that he was a crony of Gov. Thomas E. Dewey.

In all his years of broadcasting, Thomas has lost his temper only once. In 1945, during a tour of Europe, he went on the air after inspecting the Nazi death-camp at Buchenwald. Listeners who heard that broadcast say that if Thomas wanted to he could be one of the most stirring orators of our day.

Proof of Thomas' impact upon his radio audience was offered in 1938 when Newcomb Carlton, chairman of the board of directors of Western Union, offered to transmit, free of charge, any telegrams that listeners might want to send to Thomas. Carlton expected a few thousand wires, at most. But 262,490 poured in, all filled with expressions of admiration for the Demosthenes of Quaker Hill.

One Nebraska listener summed up the relationship quite succinctly when she wired: "I like you."

His news objectivity and passion for facts are well-known in the industry. "Ask Lowell for his views on pasteurized milk and he'll tell you an anecdote about Pasteur," a contemporary relates.

To MY FRIEND
Lowell Thomas
— A GENTLEMAN OF THE HIGHWAY
WITH ALL THE BEST
Rip.
4-26

"So long until Tomorrow"

Lowell Thomas
RECEIVED
266,000 TELEGRAMS

Lowell, among other things holds the all-time record for public response to a single radio program.

He was swamped by 265,654 telegrams.

Admiral Byrd in 1934 was exploring the Antarctic. Lowell was receiving intermittent personal reports from him by short wave from "Little America." A radio station at Lyttleton, New Zealand then relayed on via Postal Telegraph. Several times Lowell mentioned these on the air and gave credit to Mackey Radio, a subsidiary of Postal.

One day his phone rang. It was Newcomb Carlton, president of Western Union who said, "Why, oh why, do you keep mentioning that other outfit and never mention Western Union?"

"Let's talk it over," replied Lowell.

They met for lunch, later toured the Western Union building in Lower Manhattan. Lowell was fascinated.

"It was as near organized chaos as the Wall Street Stock Exchange. Girls on padded roller skates; baskets zooming overhead; machines creating a hum. I decided right there to bring my micro-

Novelist Homer Cory, Lowell and colleague Prosper Buranelli, with boxed avalanche of 265,654 telegrams an all-time record for responses to a single radio program. (See story on opposite page.)

phone down and broadcast from there. Perfect sound effects for my show.

"Jimmy Wallington was the announcer and Mr. Carlton told him to say that if any of my friends would like to send in a personal message, to go ahead, Western Union would pay the bill."

No one was prepared for the deluge.

Several thousand even sent their message by Postal and Western Union paid for those, too.

One man wired Lowell five chapters of the Bible, just to see if it would go through. It did.

Lowell had all quarter-of-a-million responses neatly bundled and stored in a frame building thinking some day he'd read and answer all of them. But before he could do so, he loaned the building to a group of editors who were starting a new magazine. One day a fire broke out, and all were destroyed.

So, if you were one of the 265,654, that's why you never got an answer.

I MISSED THE REPTILE AND RAN AWAY
AS FAST AS I COULD!

SECTION 7

The following Newsweek Magazine *article followed that record breaking television success with the High Adventure series, based on expeditions to Tibet, New Guinea, Timbuktu, the Arctic and other little known parts of the globe.*

Another long television series, "The World of Lowell Thomas" was recently launched by The British Broadcasting Corporation, and Odyssey Film Productions of New York.

The Newsweek *article was a 'staff' production and carried no byline, although Lowell suspects that a* Newsweek *editor who had been associated with Lowell Jr. could have been responsible.*

The profile appeared in 1957.

On and On Into Adventure

By *NEWSWEEK* STAFF

An average-looking man with thick, graying hair, and a pencil-thin mustache stood, not long ago, before an uncharted section of steaming New Guinea jungle. Behind him, a few half-civilized native guards waited with ready rifles. From the side came the muted whirr of a 35-millimeter movie camera. Before him, partly hidden by lush vegetation, a tribe of naked, ocher-painted cannibals watched him closely. Their arrows trembled slightly in taut bows. The interloper stared calmly back. Then one savage blinked, lowered his bow, eased out of the bush, and stood quietly by the man's side. The others followed. Once again, in a long career of facing similar dangers, Lowell Thomas had done the undone.

"I don't know what danger is, really," Thomas said last week, the morning after 25 million viewers had witnessed this scene in "Headhunters of New Guinea" on TV. "I've been having adventures like that all my life."

This year, with the inauguration of his TV series, the stern-faced adventurer is undergoing his busiest year in a lifetime of making an industry out of sight-seeing. He has written his 45th book. He is active in the immensely successful Cinerama movie process. His daily radio newscast is in its 28th year. Having caught and held for 40 years the eye and ear of a country historically quick to tire of public personalities, Thomas's current project, his initial safari into the TV jungle, is the acid test. Loss of popularity can be cruelly quick on TV.

The New Guinea show was the first in a new, monthly, color-film series on CBS-TV titled simply "High Adventure With Lowell Thomas." In the months to come, stay-at-homes will see films of Thomas in wild, obscure spots all over the world. Each show has a $250,000 budget. To film them, Thomas and a twenty-man crew will have traveled more than 100,000 miles.

"It has been a nightmare," one Thomas associate said last week.

"Tommy spent three weeks in New Guinea, two at the North Pole, two in Venezuela, and he'll eventually get to the Sahara, Nepal, and the desert of Northern Australia. It's incredible how a man of 65 can take such a beating."

The man who has made a career of getting into and out of dangerous and inaccessible places has survived despite one colleague's opinion that "he's the world's worst driver, and he couldn't fix a household appliance if his life depended upon it." The exotic foods of the world, within arm's reach at a thousand festive boards he has sat down to around the globe, have meant little to him because, as another associate says, "he doesn't eat much—and whatever he does eat just tastes like ham and eggs to him. He takes a drink now and then, but only for sociability. He's always exercising—that's his preference. If he isn't playing golf, he's skiing. Keeps him in good shape."

Like all his ventures, Thomas's TV series is a triumph of seemingly amateur enthusiasm over the techniques of usually sophisticated, high-style professions.

His books of adventure and biography, for example, are not generally considered hallowed contributions to the world of belles-lettres. But they have sold thousands of copies.

His early synchronized film travels in the '20s and '30s were known to have too much Thomas and not enough travel for some people's taste (some critics said the same of last week's TV debut). But they broke an impressive roster of long-run records on many of the then-narrow screens of the world.

Movie critics have described his recent participation in Cinerama as merely the work of a happy wanderer who, when things cool down at the box office, simply throws another travelogue on the fire. But to date, Cinerama with its giant, slightly three-dimensional, triptych screen has played to 32 million people around the globe.

His news show has been called uninformative, overly folksy. But many parts of the U.S., particularly the rural areas, consider Lowell Thomas the country's No. 1 newscaster. For this show alone, he gets $375,000 a year.

Thomas has never had a commercial flop. By common consent, the secret of his success is an ability to play the part of Everyman in the wilderness. In every medium Thomas finds himself, he communicates a kind of gosh-almighty feeling that (1) the world is his oyster, (2) it contains many nicely turned pearls, and (3) they can be shared by anyone who cares to read, watch, or hear Lowell Thomas.

Even his famous radio sign-off, "So long until tomorrow," carries the assumption that everybody listening today will indeed be listening tomorrow. And very noticeably, they do.

During his 65 years, Lowell Jackson Thomas has probably been heard by more people than any other man in history, and he has unquestionably offered the world the greatest variety of sight and word pictures. By so doing, he has also acquired, several times over, the comfortable bank balance and fixed assets of a twentieth-century millionaire.

His home is a 27-year-old, 34-room brick Colonial set on 3,000 acres of rolling countryside at Quaker Hill, N.Y. The house is surrounded by woodland containing two bass-stocked lakes, an 800-foot run for skiing (a sport that has cost Thomas uncounted broken bones), wild deer, a steel platform from which five states are clearly visible on crisp autumn days, a four-car garage, a broadcasting studio, and a root cellar holding a film library and potatoes.

Like a successful banker, he is surrounded by a domestic and professional staff of eleven, many of whom have been with him for twenty years or more. His dress, however, belies the banker's taste. On one crisp autumn day last week, for example, Thomas was, like the five states, clearly visible from a distance. Wearing a green shirt, a red tie, a blue sweater, and a Western hat (gallon dimensions a trifle less than 10), Thomas tried to squeeze his far-ranging life into a few minutes' talk.

"I had been a reporter in Chicago," he said. "That was after my childhood days working in the Cripple Creek gold mines of Colorado. When America entered World War I, I was sent by the War Department on a tour of the allied fronts to get material and movies that would explain to the United States just what was going on over there. I covered the French, English, Belgian, and American armies on the Western Front. Then I went to the Near East.

"I was in Jerusalem one day when I met a young Oxford archeologist named T. E. Lawrence. He had become bored with his job, and he was in the process of stirring up the Bedouins to fight against their old enemies, the Turks. I had the only camera in Arabia, and I was the only reporter to get his story. I covered his campaign and Comdr. Edmund H. H. Allenby's capture of Jerusalem, the last crusade. They were the luckiest things that could have happened to me. No one had ever heard of Lawrence of Arabia or Allenby, and they were fascinated with what I had to tell them. When I found people being so enthralled, I toured the world with a film show. 'With Lawrence of Arabia and Allenby in Palestine,' I called it, and it was a tremendous success."

From the tour and the publication of his first book, "With Lawrence in Arabia," Thomas made his first million dollars in a year. Then, because he had given the show 3,000 times, he swore never to speak in public again. He and his wife, Frances, spent the next decade traveling around the world—they stopped counting after 100 sea voyages—and writing adventure books.

In 1930, Floyd Gibbons, the dashing one-eyed reporter and correspondent and then the only regular newscaster on radio, lost that distinction the day after he insulted his sponsor's wife. CBS board chairman William S. Paley, seeking a replacement, heard from a man who had once attended a Thomas travel lecture in London. After a fifteen-minute tryout, Thomas was hired back into the public-speaking business. He has been doing the same radio news show ever since.

"I still think radio is a better medium for disseminating news than TV," Thomas said, "because most news is mental, not pictorial. I feel that people like a disembodied voice better than having to watch a Brooks Brothers face reading off the news on TV."

Thomas returned to the realm of feature-length films in 1952, soon after attending a showing of the Cinerama process. "I was stunned when I first saw it," he said. "Until then, every Hollywood mogul had looked it over, said 'Wow,' and left without knowing what to do with it. When I saw it, I knew exactly what to do with it because I had the travel history behind me. I brought it out of the laboratory where it had been for fourteen years. We raised the money and there have been five Cinerama shows to date.

"I have never cared what the critics say, especially about Cinerama. They resent this bastard form of entertainment. They say 'Where's the plot? Where's the love story?' They don't realize, apparently, that we're reaching the audiences. We've smashed records everywhere. Until Cinerama came along, 'Gone With the Wind' had grossed the most money of any film [$40 million], and it played in 50,000 theaters to do it. Now the Cinerama shows are ahead, and we use only 22 theaters around the world. It is not so important to me, now that I've fooled around with it, and now that the TV show is under way."

"Except for a little newscasting before World War II, I've stayed away from TV. I knew it would bring me into town, and I hate towns. I like the hills. But General Motors, my radio sponsor, told me: 'You somehow have a lease on public life that we never anticipated. We want you to do a TV show for us.' Well when your sponsor asks you, it's hard not to go along. I said I would if I could do what I liked and with an almost unlimited budget. They agreed, and we started 'High Adventure.'

"I don't know how the sponsor feels, but I'm prepared, if they want it, to do shows like this for ten years. I've been every place except Paraguay and Siberia, and I hope to present them all to the public.

"I'd like to go back to Tibet, of course. The first time, I broke my leg on the way out over the Himalayas and wouldn't have come out of it but for the help of my son, Lowell Jr. I'd like to do New Guinea again. The trip I took for the first TV show was in the lowlands. The humidity was awful and we lost a lot of film and part of the sound track. I hate humidity. I hate flies. I'd like to take a crew up into the uncontrolled highlands. Southern Alaska is another one of my favorite places—Glacier Bay and the section where the mountains rise higher from the sea than any other place in the world."

As a man whose travels have brought him into the world of diplomats, soldiers of fortune, and royalty, Thomas drops names with commanding unintention. "The Duke of Windsor is a charming fellow. We went on a tiger hunt once in India and we were the only two parties left in Venice when the Germans and Austrians were outside the city gates . . . I had General Vandenberg working on a special trip for me . . . Stu Symington was a help too . . . Dick Nixon played my golf course here . . . Last night, I had a call at 3 a.m. from Finn Ronne in Antarctica. Wanted to tell me he's naming a mountain range after me down there."

With Lowell Jr., left, accompanied by three Tibetan noblemen in the Forbidden City of Lhasa. The thousand-roomed Potala in the background, with its golden domes. Year: 1949.

En route back to civilization from inner Tibet, he had one of his close "calls" on a lofty pass when a horse wheeled and spun him onto the rocks, breaking his hip in eight places. With no doctors, he was carried for 20 days around canyon walls, over rocky trails, and over the Himalayas to India. Within a year he was back skiing on Alaskan glaciers.

With Lowell Jr. in Tibet. Referring to his injury, Lowell says simply, "Without my son I never would have made it!"

Memories of Lhasa, Tibet, in 1963 when he met again with the Dalai Lama, now in exile on the Indian side of the Himalayas. They have remained friends, with Lowell the head of Tibetan relief in America.

Since that first Alaskan expedition at age of 22, he had been interested in the polar regions. Here with a Who's-Who of Arctic exploration, right at the North Pole: Bernt Balchen (polar and trans-Atlantic flier), Admiral Donald Mac Millan (last surviving member of Peary's North Pole expedition), Lowell Jr. and Sir Hubert Wilkins of Arctic and Antarctic fame.

He has made several trips to the South Pole. Here shaking hands there with USN Rear Admiral James R. Reedy, then in command of Operation Deep Freeze, and more recently in command of U.S. carriers in the China Sea off Viet Nam.

Gonzalez Studio

Famed Arctic explorer and author Peter Freuchen with Lowell Thomas shortly before departure for North Pole. Freuchen died next day virtually in Lowell's arms, after 1957 expedition had reached Alaskan jumping-off point.

Explorers Club award is presented to the distinguished Polar explorer, Viljahlmur Stefansson, by Honorary President of Club.

He has been going back and forth to Alaska for more than 50 years, making his first adventure film there in 1914.

Three distinguished American explorers: Admiral Richard E. Byrd, Lowell, and Roy Chapman Andrews.

Mitchel B. Lenley

In 1957, on a trip to New Guinea for his TV High Adventure series, posing with a group of cannibals who had recently dined on their neighbors.

The Fifties also saw a return to the desert sands. This time, the lower Sahara and the fabled city of Timbuktu.

L.T. in front of History of Civilization fireplace, holding stone from Berlin wall and tile from Peking Temple of Heaven; Mason Michael Pagnetti, with Mayan stone image, about to be installed.

Lowell Thomas' New York office. The red books are his broadcasts for the past 38 years. Above are paintings of the Seven Wonders of the World, by Mario Larrinaga.

Hammersley Hill, named for the early colonial family to whom this area was a grant from Queen Anne, more than two hundred years ago.

Frances Thomas, with Cloverbrook in the background, their first home on Quaker Hill. (Painting by Gene Anthony.)

Lowell Thomas Jr. as Colonel of the Knickerbocker Greys.—
Painting by McClelland Barclay.

Lowell Thomas Jr., in Tibetan outfit. In background Tibetan
Buddhist silk, "tanka."

Boyhood home of Lowell Thomas. Now a museum of his momentos at Victor, Colorado.

The historical mining town of Victor, Colorado. The town of Victor, heart of the Cripple Creek District, once famous mining center and now a growing recreational area.

Since World War II, L.T. has led many expeditions for his TV High Adventure series and other film presentations. Here he is on 1953 trip.

Up the Sepik River, in New Guinea, for TV series. Year: 1957.

The producer of Cinerama before one of the original Seven Wonders of the World. His wide-screen films with stereophonic sound revolutionized the motion picture world of the Fifties and later.

With Rear Admiral James Reedy at Capetown prior to first trans-Antarctic flight from Africa to Australasia. October, 1963.

Among other activities promoting skiing, he is on hand for the annual Lowell Thomas Classic at Utah's Treasure Mountain. With trophy are skiier Tim Hayden, left, and Woody Anderson, general manager at the Park City area.

Observing his 75th birthday after a morning tour of Alta's ski slopes.

L.T. swinging down Germania, at Alta, Utah, famous for that "deep powder."

SECTION 8

Aside from his family, two of L.T.'s enthusiasms in recent years have been SKIING and GOLFING!

Witness: Lowell is one of the best known and most familiar figures on ski slopes—wherever there is any skiing. Trails and races have been named for him and a year ago he was elected to The Ski Hall of Fame.

Two sketches make up this section: the first, by poet George Carroll, "Snow Long 'Til Tomorrow," ran serially in Ski Magazine, in the winter of 1957. The second, "Flags in the Front Yard," was printed in 1957, in Sports Illustrated.

Snow Long Until Tomorrow

By GEORGE CARROLL *Author and poet.*

According to informed sources, well over three million Americans—some say five—now call themselves skiers, without doing violence to the basic verities. What violence many of them do to their own basic anatomy is another matter.

The point is that, little over a decade ago, a researcher in the field would have settled for a small fraction of this figure. And two decades ago there was nothing to research. The sport has grown like crazy.

This skiing group is nothing if not democratic. It cuts across social barriers, income brackets, political parties and religious persuasions. If Death is the final great leveler, skiing does very well in the interim. What's more, our three million plus is made up of men, women and children of just about every age, residing in just about every state in the union. Every age? Yes, from two-year-olds to that eighty-year-older, Panama Canal engineer Smith-Johannsen who still takes a ten-mile ski jaunt in stride.

And the best friend any of them have is a dynamic, dark-haired man known to millions of radio listeners as America's most famous newsman.

Nobody but nobody loves skiers like Lowell Thomas loves them. And few have done more to extend their pleasure geographically as well as vertically, or, in general, to spread the gospel of their special cult. If, as Otto Schneibs is supposed to have been the first to say, skiing is a way of life, Lowell Thomas lives it up at a furious pace. And keeps quite a few boon companions living it up with him.

A growing number of individuals and corporations today exhibit varying degrees of fondness for this skiing horde. But in most cases the love affair carries at least a taint of the commercial. The profit motive raises its ugly head behind the snowbank.

It would appear that when the famous broadcaster has ventured into these circles it has been more for the fun of it than with intent to make a buck! In skiing's earlier days, several good friends —Roland Palmedo and "Jay" Cooke among them—invited Lowell to help finance New England's first chair lift on Mt. Mansfield, at Stowe, Vt. A few years back these gentlemen, all but L. T., sold out to the present fairy godfather of the Vermont area—Cornelius V. Starr from Shanghai, Hongkong, and points East, West, North and South. Presumably they received some return on their investment! Meanwhile, their chair lift had brought them, and thousands of others, a great deal of wonderful skiing fun. Lowell stayed in because he didn't want to get out. And, in like manner, he is involved in the development of a few more mountains, in Colorado, in Maine, and even in Austria, at St. Anton, birthplace of downhill skiing. Two ski clubs, one east and one west, were launched by him.

Even among the simon-purists, it is doubtful if anyone can surpass the Thomasian record for the sheer diversity of help he has given, and continues to give, the ski sport.

Has someone come up with a new site for a development? Does he need encouragement in pushing it along? Send emissaries posthaste to Pawling, N. Y. Is the Olympic Fund faltering? Does John Clair's ICC need help? Lowell's your man! A magic name on the printed appeal; a persuasive speaker at tonight's rally, tomorrow's luncheon. Or perhaps you fancy yourself another John Jay? You've got the makings of a great ski film, if only enough people will look at it. The answer is simple. Find someone who knows someone who can get the ear and the eye of the famous radio and film commentator. If he can't help you, no one can. If you have written a book on winter sports the odds are the intro is by L. T.

Some time ago, acting on the assumption that what had proved good for others might prove good for us too, your correspondent wangled an invitation to Pawling. We arrived on a perfect autumn afternoon. There being no snow in sight we were not surprised to find our host concentrating on the sport he loves second best. Golf. In the company of a gimlet-eyed gentleman who turned out to be his manager, Mr. Frank Smith, Mr. Thomas was lashing away at his private twelve-hole course. Why twelve? That's another story.

"Excuse please," we ventured politely, "if you fellows can stop gloating over the millions you're making on Cinerama, we would like to talk skiing."

Both men fixed us with a dour look. "The shoe is on the other foot," my host said firmly. Mr. Smith here is bemoaning the high cost of maintaining this golf course. However, fire away!"

We proceeded to fire. Where—we asked, since it seemed best to start at the beginning—where had Lowell Thomas first strapped on a pair of skis?

The answer was during World War I. Lowell was then a war correspondent attached to the Italian *alpini*. They were holding a line high in the snow-covered Alps separating northern Italy from Austria.

"It was there," up at 13,000 feet on Monte Rosa, my host explained, "that skiing and I first met. For quite a while, the romance— if you wish to call it that—was rather one-sided. I liked skiing. But there was some doubt that skiing liked me."

The future, as the song has it, is not ours to see. Across the intervening valley, serving with the Austrian forces, was another man destined to immortality in the annals of American—indeed world— skiing. His name: Hannes Schneider. Even closer than that: the officer in command of the refugio where a basket cableway had dropped L. T., a captain in the Italian ski troops, was still another colorful personality soon to be identified with skiing's early days in this country, but especially in Canada. This one? That all, ramrod-straight, devil-may-care scion of Russian and Italian nobility, the Marquis degli d'Albizzi, known to skiers as "the Markee."

Lowell Thomas' first skiing for fun did not come until some years after the war. And the place? "Right here, on these rolling slopes of Quaker Hill." It was, he further recalled, early January, 1926. Thomas had recently made a speaking tour of Canada. (Incidentally, the word "lecture" is one of his verbal taboos. Too stuffy.) By now, he was no longer the unknown war correspondent. He had acquired wide fame, a substantial fortune.

Lowell Thomas was the biographer, discoverer really, of those two glamorous figures of World War I, Lawrence of Arabia and Count Luckner, the Sea Devil. Lowell's films, accompanied by his personal commentary, on Colonel Lawrence had proven a worldwide sensation. In London, his show ran for a year and broke all attendance records, first at Covent Garden Royal Opera House and then the huge Royal Albert Hall. His book *Lawrence of Arabia* became a whopping best-seller. His cussess with the German sea raider was equally spectacular. He was now in great demand as a public speaker, and already the Thomas home at Pawling was becoming a mecca for all manner of important and interesting vistors.

In Montreal, Lowell had purchased three pairs of skis and ski poles. There was a special reason behind this investment. Mr. and Mrs. Thomas were preparing to entertain their first visiting royalty. No less a personage than Prince Wilhelm, second son of the then King Gustav of Sweden.

"I told myself," says Lowell "that here was an opportunity I must not miss. A rare chance to get some pointers on skiing from one who came from the very cradle of the sport!"

Alas, it did not work out that way. This particular Swedish prince hadn't even an academic interest in skiing. His all-absorbing passion was equatorial Africa! He had stopped off at Pawling following an expedition to the Congo. Finding mid-January in Dutchess County much too cold, His Royal Highness rarely left the house during the ten days of his visit.

"I did manage to get in a little skiing with Prince Wilhelm's aide, a captain in the Swedish army," says Lowell. "Having skied from early boyhood, the captain was an expert on cross-country, and he gave me my first lesson in that."

But he had to wait quite a while for his first formal instruction in the sport. Several years in fact. It was the historic winter of 1932, and the scene was Lake Placid, N. Y., where the only Winter Olympic Games yet held in this country were in progress.

A tall, handsome Norwegian, Erling Strom, was serving as ski instructor to the members and guests of the Lake Placid Club. Inspired by the skiing of those two Norwegian champions, Birger and Sigmund Ruud, Lowell Thomas signed up for lessons. It proved to be more than his first professional tutelage. For pupil and instructor it marked the beginning of a close and long-lasting friendship. For twenty-four years they have been skiing together. It was at Lake Placid too that Lowell formed another friendship and found a boon skiing companion for the future. The one with the late Hubert Stevens, Olympic bobsled champion, amateur sportsman, and one of the creators of the Whiteface Mountain Ski Development in the Adirondacks. In fact it was Lowell who lured Hubert away from the bob run, and for many years they toured the mountains of North America.

It is a characteristic of Lowell Thomas that he never stops trying to learn more about anything that interests him. Certainly this has been true of his skiing. "Over the years," he will tell you, "I have sat at the feet—no pun intended!—of the most learned professors in the business." Would he name some of them? He would.

When Katherine Peckett of Sugar Hill started the "Austrian invasion" to New Hampshire and Cannon Mountain, Lowell and Lowell, Jr., went there to learn the Arlberg technique from Sig Buchmayr, Kurt Thalhammer, Otto Lang and all the others who taught at Franconia. Next came weekends with Benno Rybizka at Jackson, N.H., and Tuckerman Ravine on Mt. Washington. There was, of course, the late great Hannes Schneider, for whose genius American skiing is forever indebted to the memory of a man named Harvey Gibson. It was Gibson's influence in international banking circles which finally secured Schneider's release from a Nazi concentration camp. Lowell was one of the first to welcome him at North Conway, along with Herbert Schneider, Toni Matt and many more.

After that, and the list is endless, he skied with Jacques Charmoz, Sepp Ruschp, Lionel Hayes, Kerr Sparks, Otto Hollaus, Bruce Fenn, and others at Stowe, before and after the Mansfield chair lift was built. He skied with Friedl Pfeifer, Hans Hauser, Luggi Foegger, Sigi Engl, Otto Steiner, Wiggi Hasher, Dick Durrance, the Engens, Alf, Sverre and Corey, Steve Brandley, Bill Klein, and a score of others in the west. In the east, he accompanied such European stars as Emile Allais, Sepp Froelich, Raidar Anderson, Tom Murstad and Heinrich Harrer on their first ski jaunts in this country.

Others who added fire to his early enthusiasm were Peter Gabriel, Johnny Litchfield, Michael Fuersinger, Fritz Wiessner, Sel Hannah, and some of his most constant companions, Chris and Mary Young, Jim Parker and "Iron Man" Bob Kehoe and Jack and Gladys Sawyer. The list is literally endless.

Would the commentator name his favorite? Put one above the other? Not Lowell. "Each of these," he averred, "is an expert in his own way. Each has his own personality, his own way of imparting knowledge of the sport."

Then what about equipment, we asked next. Here again the Thomas taste seems all-inclusive. "I suspect I'd be better off with only one pair of skis, instead of a dozen. Most of mine are of standard makes. But some are experimental, and I even have a pair of 'goonies'—the sawed off variety for clowning. Did you ever see Prince Bernhard go whirling by on his? Or Jimmy Madden of Boston who is the original wizard on 'goonies'? It's both funny and spectacular."

A dozen pairs. But not many skiers were that well equipped. What, if any advice would he offer the person who must limit himself to one, or at most, two pairs of skis? And what of bindings—safety or otherwise?

Here again, the nation's most notable amateur was reluctant to take sides. As it was with teaches, he said, so with equipment. You do best with what suits you best. Of course, privately he may tell you, or advise you whom to consult. As for safety bindings—sure, a fine thing. Sometimes he uses them, sometimes he doesn't. He has broken bones both with and without.

From Lake Placid, Lowell tried Sugar Hill in New Hampshire. Those early days of excitement in the snowbelt. Days of the first immortal rope tow at Woodstock . . . the pioneering Fred Pabst . . . Eastern Slopes. Those days when Kate Peckett was making ski history with her imported yodelers from the Tyrol, vanguard of the Austrian invasion that continued for years, gave tremendous impetus to skiing in America, and radically changed its emphasis. The leisurely ski touring, the ski jumping of the Scandinavians lost favor. Now everyone must learn to ski as they skied in the Austrian, Swiss and French Alps. Learn the technique of the swift, down-mountain running, the high-speed turns of the Alpine countries.

Lowell Thomas, quick to recognize the significance of the Sugar Hill importations, still gives high praise to a woman many younger skiers never heard of—Katherine Peckett. "Her vision," says the famed radio newsman, "her enterprise, gave recreational skiing a boost that sent it to dizzy heights." And of course Averill Harriman who did the same for the West when by magic he created Sun Valley.

From the start, Lowell Thomas faced a unique complication in his pursuit of skiing pleasure. Career-wise he was still dealing in his favorite commodity: the day's news. But now he made his living disseminating that news over the airwaves, coast to coast.

It was a job which assumed his presence five evenings a week within the network studio. For obvious reasons these studios are found only in the larger centers of population. For reasons equally obvious, skiing was to be found only in mountainous areas remote from the cities. All in all, it posed an interesting problem in logistics.

But the man who was not to be rebuffed by the uncommunicative genius of a Colonel Lawrence, who later was to penetrate the impenetrable Tibet, was never one to shy away from problems. This one he met head on. Perhaps he couldn't bring skiing to Radio City or to Madison Avenue. Then how about taking his broadcasting studio to the Adirondacks, the Green Mountains, the Laurentians, the Rockies, the Wasatch, the Sierras? That was precisely what he proceeded to do, and still does.

Soon the Lowell Thomas nightly newscasts were being picked up by remote control from the fashionable Lake Placid Club, from the Lodge at Smugler's Notch, from colorful Mont Tremblant, from the new and glamorous Sun Valley, from Aspen, Donner Pass, Camp Hale, Climax, Mount Hood, and even Alaska. Skiers jampacked the makeshift broadcasting room, spilled on to the platform, harassed the engineer. Ski boots tangled with wire cables and threatened to unplug the tenuous connection with the outside world. But through it all, the star performer retained his imperturability. Out went the day's news. The ringing voice of authority rang no less in Placid than in Rockefeller Plaza. The quick change of pace, the artful modulatio of tone to suit the import of the day's news, the parenthetical personals, the wryly humorous comments were still there. If anything, they took new stimulus from the day's exercise on some snowy mountainside, from a howling blizzard just beyond the improvised studio.

And at once a number of things began to happen. First off, the popular and busy commentator was able to get in a great deal of skiing which he would otherwise have had to forego. Which, of course, was the primary aim. Secondly, the ski report, the places where people ski, and the people who made skiing their business, began to get some enormously valuable, if incidental advertising on the airwaves. And lastly, a listening audience of millions began to hear a great deal about the joys and thrills of this great winter sport. One can only guess at the number of new converts thus made, but it must have been considerable.

Those Lowell Thomas radio road shows at the ski slopes are still something to see in action. In addition to the featured player, the cast includes a network engineer, a traveling secretary with the appropriate name of Electra who doubles in brass as the broadcast timer, and a telegraph operator. This is the irreducible minimum. With this there frequently goes an entourage of friends from far and wide; for Mr. Thomas is a world-renowned traveler.

Naturally, the show is not without its hazards. There was a time at Lake Placid when all the careful preparations of weeks seemed likely to go for naught. Fire, raging through the business district of a nearby town, had knocked out key trunk telephone lines. Lines which were to carry the Lowell Thomas broadcast from the Adirondacks to CBS in New York. Would the broadcast get through? No one could say. Uncertainty prevailed up to, even beyond the magic hour of 6:45 p.m. Not until the broadcast was over did Lowell have any assurance that he had not been talking merely for a hundred or so persons crowded into the room. But it had gone through. The telephone company working one of those minor miracles of last-minute hook-ups—Lake Placid to Canada to New England to somewhere else—finally to New York!

But it was in the Laurentians that the skimeister of the airwaves was treated to one of his most shaking experiences before the microphone. After a full day's skiing in the "crisp" winter air (forty below on the north side), Lowell had just started one of his nightly newscasts, this time from the beautiful Mont Tremblant Lodge. Without warning, the voice known to millions suddenly went dead. Quit. To this day, the broadcaster isn't too sure what happened. "There I was," he says, "moving along on schedule when, suddenly—silence! My lips continued to form the words, but no sounds came forth. At least no sounds that anyone could long bear listening to."

But the Thomas luck held firm. Busy with his own affairs, Lowell Thomas junior was seldom able to accompany his famous father on these skiing jaunts. But this night, by great good fortune, "Sunny" was there. Not only there, but seated at the table timing the broadcast. With one expressive gesture, Lowell senior shoved microphone and script in front of the younger man. They were on the air. Coast to coast. The younger Thomas met the emergency like the veteran trouper he was. With no more than a slightly raised eyebrow he commenced with the news where his father left off. The broadcast finished on the nose. So well had the younger man absorbed his father's intonation and mannerisms, that many in the listening audience may never have suspected that the voice they were hearing at the close was not the same voice that had opened the newscast.

It was in these same Laurentians, before Joe and Mary Ryan created Mont Tremblant, that the Lowell Thomas ski broadcasts took on a note of piquancy not equalled since. Telegraphic communications were scarce in the land of the habitant. The Canadian Pacific Railroad station at St. Jovite offered the best possibilities. Within limits. The main waiting room of the station could not be made available. But there was another possibility. There was this smaller room generally—er, ah, generally reserved for *mesdames*. It could be made available, *m'sieur*. Lowell looked at his engineer, a Canadian on that occasion. The latter, not without some trepidation, looked at the room. Will do, was the engineer's verdict.

So it came about that on various occasions, for several winters thereafter, a man who could have chosen to remain comfortably in his twenty-odd room Georgian country house on his 3,000-acre estate was content to operate from the ladies' room of a tiny railroad station high in the Province of Quebec. With his movements further restricted by the presence of a score or more of his fellow skiers, not to mention a truckload of radio equipment. Surely few men ever gave greater proof of the grip this sport can get on its adherents!

Of course, with the coming of Mont Tremblant, life in the Laurentians improved greatly for the newscaster. The Mont Tremblant story is Joe and Mary Ryan's story. (It is engagingly told in a recently published book of that title written by two skiers, John and Frankie O'Rear.) But it is a part of the Lowell Thomas story, too. Because it was Lowell who brought the man and the mountain together. With an assist from Tom and Harry Wheeler.

The meeting was to prove earth-shaking in a very literal sense. It took place back in the mid-thirties. Lowell was staying at the Wheelers' Gray Rocks Inn. From the windows of this friendly chalet, the mountain named Tremblant could be seen beckoning in the distance. With Lowell Thomas, to see a mountain is to wish that he might see it closer. They fascinate him. But this one, in the mid-thirties, was not too accessible. Tom Wheeler had an idea. He would fly his noted guest northward and land him on the frozen surface of the lake, at the base of the mountain. From that point, with climbing skins on their skis, it would not be too difficult a feat to reach the summit. Harry Wheeler volunteered to go with them as guide.

At this point a husky young man seated nearby moved over. He could not help overhearing their plans, and he was interested. Could he go along? Lowell Thomas said sure, if there was room in the plane. The young man was pleased. His name, he said, was Joe Ryan, and he was from Philadelphia.

Not without some difficulties for Ryan, who was without skins until Harry Wheeler loaned his, the skiing party reached the top of Mont Tremblant. "What a view!" exclaimed Lowell Thomas, "What a mountain!" Joe Ryan nodded. "There's just one thing wrong with this mountain," he said. "It's too darn hard to climb. But I think I'll fix that!"

Fix it he did, and the fixing made ski history. And today, if you ski Mont Tremblant, you'll experience some of your greatest thrills on the trail that Joe Ryan named for Lowell Thomas. (Parenthetically you can find some other trails named for him around the country, too, including one on Whiteface in the Adirondacks, and a ski jump on Tenderfoot Hill, near Cripple Creek, Colo. And some day, if you should venture that far, you might make a landfall at Lowell Thomas Island within the Arctic Circle, named for him by polar explorer MacMillan, or find yourself flying over the Lowell Thomas Mountains near the South Pole, placed on the Graham Land map by Antarctic explorer Captain Finn Ronne.)

Mont Tremblant is as far north as you can ski in the Laurentians. But Lowell Thomas also had a hand in founding the then farthest south ski club on the continent. It came about back in 1943 when Lowell, Jr., a lieutenant in the air force, was stationed near Tucson, Ariz. Lowell Sr., flew down to visit his son. Nearby are the snowclad peaks of the Santa Catalina Mountains rising some 9,000 feet above sea level. Surely, Thomas père told his son, surely there must be good skiing on those mountains. There was. In no time at all the Thomases were stirring up enthusiasm for a ski club. The reaction was not entirely favorable. Tucson, it seemed, had a club. The Sunshine Club. "Some of the officials," Thomas recalls, "blew their tops. Couldn't quite see the idea of promoting winter sports in an area where people came to escape snow, ice and everything associated with it."

But the ski club was formed, and it has prospered. It is called Suaharo, for the giant cactus that grows thereabout. Among the things that made it unique was the impressive roster of officials and honorary members. These included such personages as Dick Durrance; Art Devlin, at that time national ski jumping champion; Hal Burton, skier and writer; Brad Washburn, noted mountaineer; Hannes Schneider; Otto Lang; Alf Engen; Erling Strom; Bill Eldred, publisher of SKI; Darryl Zanuck; and threescore or more of the top personalities of the ski world.

Incidentally, Lowell Thomas, Jr., is no mean skier himself, was beginning to make a record in competitive skiing when the war interrupted everything. A ski jumper as well as a downhill man, he won his gold medal in the former sport while a student at Dartmouth. At age fifteen he had placed fifteenth in the national downhill championships on New Hampshire's Taft trail.

With the end of the war, the radio newscaster like countless other Americans, could resume his skiing in earnest. But, unlike many others, there was one place he could not get to. Europe. Somehow, broadcasting by shortwave doesn't satisfy sponsors, except when a war is on. But he could and did ski America first. From Mad River to Yosemite and remote Mineral King, from Manchester to Snoqualmie, Alta, the Sugar Bowl, Squaw Valley, and the unskied mountains of Colorado's San Juan. With an occasional holiday in summer, when he was free, there was still skiing to be had in such places as Chile, the Columbia icefields, the Juneau (Alaska) icecap. Lowell was soon adding all these places to his personal map of, as he puts it, "places I have skied and left my mark—sitzmark that is!"

Everywhere the famed radio figure skied, he made new enthusiasts for the sport. Movie stars, high-ranking military men, literary lights, prize-fighters, diplomats—he got them all to try it at least.

Ironically, his most highly publicized piece of proselytizing resulted in failure.

For several years Lowell Thomas had talked the joys of the ski sport to one of his neighbors at Pawling. He had used all his formidable persuasive powers. But the neighbor happened to be a particularly busy man. His name was Thomas E. Dewey and in those days he was governor of the state of New York. Opportunities to work a visit to the ski slopes into the gubernatorial schedule were few and far between. But finally, one morning Lowell got the call he had been waiting for. "Well," the governor said briskly, "I am now ready for that ski lesson you've been promising me. Let's go!"

Lowell groaned inwardly. "The governor couldn't possibly have picked a worse day," he says sadly. "His timing was terrible. It was mid-January. We had had the usual thaw followed by the usual freeze-up. Our private skiing slope, which we call Strawberry Hill, was a sheet of ice. Even Toni Matt, Ernie McCulloch or Stein Eriksen would have shunned it. Certainly no place for a beginner.

Jim Parker, that likable and versatile character whose tragic death by drowning in Pakistan last summer is mourned by all who knew him, was ski instructor at Strawberry Hill. To genial Jim went the impossible assignment of giving Governor Dewey his first lesson in the fundamentals of the sport on ice. Jim did his best. Presumably his distinguished pupil also did his best. But it was not a happy morning. "The governor," Lowell admits, "got a very dim view of skiing. Not surprising when one considers that he was viewing it from a prone position much of the time."

Did it make any difference in their friendship, we wanted to know. We don't know. At any rate Thomas E. and L. T. still seem to be friends. "However," Lowell adds, "when I am with him now, I avoid talking skiing."

If Lowell Thomas avoids talking skiing with Tom Dewey, then the former governor unwittingly acquired a new distinction. Because the squire of Pawling will go out of his way to talk skiing with anyone, any time, any place.

It was about here that we asked if he would care to mention any special thrills, near escapes and that sort of thing.

"I think of the strangest skiing trip I ever made," our host recalled, "occurred some years ago in Colorado. The superintendent of the Camp Bird mine near the town of Ouray was a skier. Hearing that I was in the vicinity he invited me to join him in what he promised would be a most unusual ski trip. He was right.

"At the appointed hour," Lowell went on, "we arrived at the mine entrance. Here, garbed in slickers and helmets, and carrying our skis, the superintendent, Lowell, Jr., and I climbed aboard a tiny mine train and were carried to a point deep inside the mountain. Here we entered a cage and were whisked to a higher level. We left this for another train-ride, followed by another ascension in a cage. We were near the top now, and we entered a long, narrow tunnel, almost impassable because of ice forming from surface water. Through this we crawled on our hands and knees, pushing our skis ahead of us. At last we emerged in brilliant sunshine, into what is called the Chicago Basin. The effect was electrifying. We found ourselves in a vast bowl at almost 14,000 feet, near the crest of the San Juan mountains. On every side stretched an expanse of snow-covered slopes as impressive as anything I had ever seen. We snapped on our skis and started down. What followed was one of the longest runs I ever made, and one of the most nerve wracking because of the accompanying roar of spring avalanches.

Sentimentally it is pleasing to know that Colorado provided our most famous recreational skier with one of his most memorable experiences. Because it was in that state, in the mountains around Cripple Creek, that Lowell Thomas spent his boyhood, for twelve years living at 10,000 ft. It remained, however, for New England to provide the terrain for what turned out to be his most satisfying skiing exploit.

The subject of this article is one of those men who refuses to pay the usual obeisance to the passage of time. Blessed with sound health, he guards that blessing. No one who did less could have achieved his record of accomplishment in so many fields—as a writer, a public speaker, a world traveler, news broadcaster, newsreel commentator and—currently—producer of the revolutionary and fabulously successful Cinerama motion picture spectacles.

But even for a Lowell Thomas, the half-century mark was something not to be dismissed lightly. And one fine day—it's a few years ago now—he awoke to the knowledge that he was fifty years old. No, that's not quite accurate. Fifty years perhaps—but not old! And to prove this, not to others but to himself, he felt there was an assignment that needed to be attended to.

For some years, Lowell had been one of the regulars on the spring pilgrimage to Tuckerman Ravine, that esoteric haunt of die-hard skiers near the summit of Mt. Washington in New Hampshire. Each spring, when snow vanishes elsewhere, and avalanches have filled the Tuckerman bowl to a depth of a hundred feet, several hundred who dread to see winter go, stripped to a minimum under the hot sun, toil into the lower reaches of this domain of ice, rock, and cyclonic wind. Having climbed to the foot of the Headwall, they spend what is left of the day climbing, side-slipping, traversing, schussing or spilling head over heels on one of the most precipitous snowfields in the east or anywhere.

While all this is going on, a handful of the more daring make their way to a dizzy shelf still farther up mountain. From that point they try their luck at running the Headwall itself. Only a hardy few tackle this, for it's a thousand-foot sheer precipice against which the midwinter snows that have avalanched off the Mt. Washington cone cling for a few brief weeks in April and May. And Lowell Thomas picked his fiftieth birthday—a day in early April—to join this band of brothers. With him for moral support were many of his skiing companions—Sepp Ruschp, Kerr Parks, Lionel Hayes, Bruce Fenn, Bob Bourdon, Otto Hollaus and Sigurd Winsness, who had escaped from Norway when the Nazis invaded his country. In fact he had fled, on skis, via Lapland and Finland, to Bolshevik Russia, and on across Siberia.

"After a rest on the summit," Lowell reminisces, "we sped down the smooth cone. Then the Headwall—over that cliff, where as you try to look over and pick a route, it's so steep you can't even see the section of the wall just below you. For the first 200 feet, no trouble. Then, a crevasse. I don't quite know what happened. But in a flash I was going end over end. A fall that continued for the remaining 800 feet. Once you lose your balance on the Tuckerman Headwall there isn't a thing you can do about it. Anyhow, I had proved a point, whatever it was."

It was a bruised and slightly befuddled radio commentator who finally spun to a stop far down at the foot of the wall. Which is one way to celebrate attainment of the half-century mark.

By far the worst accident to befall the noted broadcaster, in a lifetime of adventuring off the beaten path, involved mountains but no skiing—the highest mountains in the world. It deserves passing mention here if only because it cost him, among other things, the loss of a full winter's skiing fun.

It happened on the homeward leg of that history-making journey into Tibet which the two Lowells, father and son, made in the summer of 1950. They had left the forbidden city of Lhasa far behind. The border of northern India was a two-week trail journey ahead. And it was at this point that, while crossing 17,000-foot Karo La, that Lowell senior had the misfortune to be tossed by a half-broken Tibetan horse that whirled just as he was in the act of mounting. He landed on some rocks and was knocked out. The fall, as X-rays taken some twenty days later, in India, established, broke his right hip in eight places, rendering him a helpless cripple.

The remainder of that journey out to civilization must have been a Tibetan nightmare. In all probability it would have killed a man of less stamina, less determination to live. Lowell Thomas survived it. But he takes no credit for this himself. That he came out alive, he will tell you, was due to his son who pulled him through that first cold night. And after that due to the persistence, the improvisation and unfailing optimism of Lowell junior, on whom command of the expedition at once devolved. This was in September. But by the end of October, having been carried for twenty days on the shoulders of Tibetans across rivers, around mountain walls, and over the main range of the Himalayas, and then flown by stages to New York, and there operated on successfully by one of the leading orthopedic surgeons of our time, Lowell was hobbling about on crutches. And that winter the FIS championships were held at Lake Placid and at Aspen, Colo. The newscaster was there. Only one thing troubled him somewhat. "I hope," a friend remembers hearing him say, "I hope I won't be taken for a ski casualty. I don't like sailing under false colors."

By summer he had thrown away his crutches and was off on an expedition to an icefield in Alaska. Back on skis again.

But he became a ski casualty soon enough. Albeit a minor one. The following winter he broke the other leg. On that Tuckerman Headwall? The Nose Dive? Bell Mountain? Not at all. Ironically it happened right on his own slope. On gentle Strawberry Hill at Pawling. Lowell was giving a few pointers to a beginner, on unbreakable crust. But at the transition point near the bottom of the slope, a ski broke through—and there he was again!

All of which of course did nothing to dampen the enthusiasm of the Great Enthusiast.

Except on the ski slope, the golf course or in similar personal equations, to speak of Lowell Thomas has long meant to speak of something more than the individual. Nothing less than a sizable and highly efficient organization could handle the multiple and far-ranging interests of this extraordinary man.

To begin with there is the office in New York. Here reigns Mary Davis, most seraphic of the famed Seraphic Secretaries, as they call themselves, a quite special group of these young ladies who run things in New York. Quaker Hill has its own office, with complete broadcasting studio, a film projection and editing room, a theater-in-a-barn that will seat a hundred or so on main floor and balcony.

It was here that the famous introductory sequences for the first Cinerama production were shot; here John Jay and other ski filmers are often invited to try out their latest pictures. Here too, Gene and Electra Nicks, radio engineer and personal secretary respectively in the Lowell Thomas troupe, hold forth. In the background, but keeping a guiding hand on much of this, is the man whom Lowell calls his manager, Frank Smith. Smith is slight of build, with a ready smile and a deliberate way of speaking that carries more than a touch of his native Tennessee drawl. Be not deceived. Back of this amiable front is a first-rate intelligence, a capacity for quick decision and an instinct for the sound investment. All of which must prove invaluable in a job Frank Smith obviously enjoys to the hilt.

The Lowell Thomas voice has long been familiar to millions. The face that goes with it is almost as widely known. But the man himself remains largely a mystery even to those who know him best. Gregarious as he most certainly can be, the famed newscaster has a basic reticence which is, one suspects, more than the protective shield all celebrities erect against a prying public. A man who makes his living talking, Thomas is at the same time one of the great listeners. Here's a man who really *listens* to you. More, a man who remembers what he has heard.

Perhaps none of this is very surprising when one recalls that the skier, the explorer, the radio commentator and the Cinerama producer is first of all one of the great reporters of our time. A master of the quick, incisive question, of the verbal probe penetrating to the heart of the discussion. And in discussion, the Thomas interests range far and wide. He seems to retain a lifelong curiosity about everything, inherited from an erudite father. Yet for all his interest in such static things as books and conversation, Lowell Thomas remains at heart the doer. A man for whom, happily, there will always be more worlds to conquer.

So too, one feels, he remains the believer. The optimist. One assumes it is not by accident that among the scores of fascinating mementos decorating the walls of the Hammersley Hill studio, the solitary note of religion is expressed in an exquisite fragment of stained glass adjacent to the owner's desk. It is that ever-sustaining scene from the New Testament—Christ calming the waves for his frightened disciples. And the inscription? *Why Are Ye Fearful, O Ye of Little Faith?*

133

If Lowell Thomas did not find that collector's item for himself, whoever put it there knew his man.

Among the things that Thomas the skier has long regretted is the slowness of his home state of New York in providing the kind of skiing areas now so much in demand. But this winter there are signs and portents indicating that the Empire State may be on the move. For one thing, in Averell Harriman òf Sun Valley fame, the state has one of the few skiing governors in the country. Secondly, a new legislative committee, believed to be the first of its kind, has been formed to study the winter tourist situation. Half a dozen interested groups are at work surveying possible sites for new ski developments. Lowell Thomas has watched all this with special interest. He has expressed a willingness to help the state in any way practical.

As recently as a few weeks ago, at the big house on Hammersley Hill, the matter of Squaw Valley and the 1960 Winter Olympics came to the fore. More than one among those present shook their heads pessimistically. Doubt was expressed that the Californians could create the required facilities on schedule. "They'll do it!" Lowell Thomas said firmly. 'And they'll do it easily. Just wait and see."

The sole uncharacteristic note in this characteristic expression of faith and optimism is found in the final phrase, *wait and see.* Over a life-time crammed with adventure, Lowell Thomas has seen far more than most men. But waiting? That's something else. Skiing's best friend has usually been in too much of a hurry—too impatient to do much waiting. Well, maybe in the lift line. But maybe not even there. Maybe he's a director of the outfit that owns the thing! Ex-Cowhand Lowell Thomas finds his private golf course is a great place to herd celebrities.

He often broadcasts from his favorite skiing spots. Here at Sun Valley, with Hollywoodites Wendell Corey, left, Stewart Granger, right. Back left, Andrew Marton, a director of Ben Hur and many spectacular films.

Every April he skis Utah's challenging Alta slopes, with Hack Miller, sports editor of the *Deseret News*.

On Brighton ski slopes with four-way champion skiier Alf Engen.

U.S. Forest Service avalanche experts, at Alta with avalanche dog "PIF" (named for Precipitation Intensity Factor). Monty Atwater, left; Ed LaChappelle, right; Lowell, prone.

Flags In the Front Yard

By PAUL O'NEIL *SPORTS ILLUSTRATED staff writer.*

Owning a private golf course is a little like owning a private Hudson River excursion steamer, or a private operating table, or a private mallet locomotive and 50 private refrigerator cars; once you've got the thing you must figure out what to do with it. There is probably nobody in the U.S. better fitted to solve this problem than Lowell Thomas, the radio newscaster, who is the proud owner of the little (80 acres) course pictured on these pages. Thomas has devoted a great deal of his life to what might be described as the care and handling (and, at times, the creation) of celebrities; he has a sort of cattleman's knack of turning them into his corral on command and of moving among them at will without being gored. The private golf course affords him wonderful opportunities for grouping and exercising them, and there have been days when he has been able to ride his private electric caddie cart among some very impressive specimens of American longhorn.

Even so, there are times when he is a little startled at finding poles with little flags on them in plain sight of the front door of his house near Pawling, N. Y. This is unusual, for the rarity of private golf courses is only partially induced by the financial outlay which they involve. A man who is not a grass lover and a tree inspector by nature could hardly be expected to saddle himself with acres of both; conversely, he could be a sod-happy as a mole and keep the lid on his id by simply buying a farm, or a private cemetery and headstone works. Some vast, motivating urge must obviously be necessary in most cases; the late Comedian Joe Cook, for instance, liked laughs and burned to shoot a hole in one and was thus moved to construct a green shaped like a funnel. The Thomas course, however, came as a kind of afterthought in a life devoted to achieving simple princeliness and is so mixed up in his mind with innumerable other projects that he tends to classify it with his softball diamond, his local ski tow, his international fireplace (stones from all parts of the world), his stand of small dawn sequoias (from deepest Yunan province) and, at times (while on "expeditions"), to forget all about it.

Building the course, it should be explained, was easy enough—he already had 80 acres of rolling meadowland around his home and the men and machinery to keep it in shape. Laying the foundation upon which it rests, however, was another matter; Thomas built his baronial establishment out of nothing more solid than air, and did so when more orthodox American grandees were sliding into obscurity by the hundreds on the banana peel of the Great Depression. One of these was a man named Fred F. French—who got enormously rich during the 1920s by building skyscrapers in New York—and Thomas still feels indebted to him both for his grandiose concepts and his lack of foresight.

At the height of the great boom after World War I, French decided to establish a family seat worthy of his stature and accomplishments. He found the site at Quaker Hill, a lovely section of elevated forest and farm land near the Connecticut line, 75 miles north of New York City. He bought up thousands of acres of it, then tore down all the farmhouses included in his domain, planted long vistas of Norway spruce, and built, at a cost of $400,000, a great, 15-bathroomed Georgian house. When it was done, he was able to stand before it and remark that everything the eye could see was his. He went broke almost immediately and died shortly thereafter of angina pectoris.

Meanwhile, Thomas—an Army doctor's son who had grown up at Cripple Creek, Colo., had punched cattle, sampled the academic offerings of four colleges, and had gotten a start in life as a cub reporter in Cripple Creek—was proving that a man could get rich as quickly by talking as by plunging in the market or drilling oil wells. He held millions of Britons spellbound with an illustrated account on Lawrence of Arabia (whom he had cannily sought out in the desert during World War I), toured the Caribbean with Germany's sea raider, Count von Luckner, became the voice of Movietone newsreel and succeeded the late Floyd Gibbons before the microphone on the first U.S. radio news program—a position of eminence which was later to bring him nearly a half million dollars a year.

He was—and still is, at 65—ferociously addicted to sport. He loved to ride, had learned to ski in Europe in 1919 (he is now associated with Insurance Tycoon C. V. Starr in operating the great ski resort at Stowe, Vt.), and decided to make the electronic age conform to his pattern of life. Although it strained his finances to the cracking point, even at Depression prices, he bought up the whole enormous French holdings at Quaker Hill and moved into the great house. Eventually, by installing radio equipment in a barnlike studio outbuilding, he arranged to do his broadcasts at home, thereby freeing himself to indulge his passion for sport and his flair for grandly steering others toward his kind of living.

The private golf course was doubtless inevitable from that point on, although Thomas kept busy at other works for some time. The new squire of Quaker Hill spurned his predecessor's policy of isolation and, although he kept a tidy 3,000 acres for himself, allowed selected supplicants (among them New York's Thomas E. Dewey and television's Edward R. Murrow) to buy land in the country around him and to be swept along in the tide of his projects and enthusiasms. In the 1930s he went mad for softball and enrolled his friends and neighbors in a team known as the Nine Old Men, which engaged in spirited battles with a team of White House correspondents and Secret Servicemen organized by President Franklin D. Roosevelt; other celebrities were also lured to the plate, among them Westbrook Pegler, Dale Carnegie, Gene Tunney and even, at one point, Babe Ruth—who struck out.

Though his softball period was quickly followed by his present golf period, Thomas was kept so busy learning—or at any rate trying to learn—the game, and mulling over its frustrations and admiring its subtleties, that he did not immediately realize that there was golfing terrain at his very door. When a friend remarked on this fact one day four years ago, Thomas responded with a lacrity; he discovered that New Hampshire horticulturist would truck in and lay pregrown greens, ordered four, had the grass cut and, in only a fortnight, was enthusiastically operating the Hammersley Hill Golf (and Hunt) Club.

He has enlarged it since. Having installed what he conceives to be the shortest hole in the world (80 yards), he laid in the longest, which is almost one-half mile from tee to green. It is now possible to play either nine or 12 holes; the first setup being known as the Vice-Presidential course and the second as the Presidential course, in celebration of the fact that Ike and Dick Nixon have both been guests at Quaker Hill. Although ex-President Herbert Hoover is also a spasmodic visitor and, in fact, smuggled a stone out of Hitler's bunker under his coat for Thomas' fireplace a few years ago, he has yet to have a hole named after him.

To demonstrate the course in action, Thomas gathered a representative group of "members" a few days ago and put them through their paces. Several professionals reported, among them the irrepressible Gene Sarazen, who prepared for action by rolling up his pants, thrusting a cigar into his mouth, making a short speech on behalf of the Wilson Sporting Goods Company, which retains him as a sort of peripatetic exhibit. Pat Hogan, a friend of ex-Governor Dewey (who sent his regrets); Robert Trent Jones, the golf course architect; Edward R. Murrow; an editor; a publisher; John P. Sawyer, a tycoon of the International Paper Company, and his wife Gladys; assorted lady golfers and a couple of neighbors from Quaker Hill composed the rest of the cast. Thomas bustled about among them as solemnly as the tournament director at the National Open, divided them into three foursomes, sent them on their way, teed off himself and then hurried to his electric caddie cart to follow with a cargo of bags.

In observing him, as the pleasant, sunny day progressed, it was impossible not to look for some covert sign of, well, satisfaction. Very few golfers have private courses, after all, and Thomas would have been only human if he had paused, somewhere along the line, and struck at least one pose. He only bustled; his air was not exactly that of a missionary among the heathen, for his guests were obviously converts already, but it would not be inaccurate to suggest that his attitude was that of a Billy Graham briefing his advance men. Golf to Thomas is something the world needs, and he was obviously a Man with Work to Do. After lunch at the studio (beer, hamburgers, salad and ice cream), he made what seemed at first to be an astounding gesture of abnegation: he suggested that better golf was possible on the nine-hole Quaker Hill course only five minutes away and asked everyone to join him there. It turned out in the end, however, that he had built it too.

Here with neighbors Edward R. Murrow and Thomas E. Dewey, and golf greats, Gene Sarazen and Sam Snead. He has built two golf courses and belongs to many clubs including Pine Valley and the Royal & Ancient of St. Andrews, Scotland.

Since his early days in Colorado, he has been a horseman. On "Nero" his wife's favorite mount—year 1935.

The "Nine Old Men" fielded in the Thirties against FDR's "Packers," a series that lasted many years.

A Dutchess County neighbor, FDR, delighted in annual softball rivalry of his "Court Packers" against L.T.'s "Nine Old Men." One of several personal letters from FDR in L.T. files.

THE WHITE HOUSE
WASHINGTON

September 7, 1939

Personal

Dear Lowell:

If you describe your team as a team of invalids, I can only tell you that my team comes directly from the emergency ward of the hospital.

In any event, it is good to know how well and truly both teams represent Dutchess County. A careful check-up shows that not one member of either team saw Dutchess County before he was fifty years old.

I fear we cannot play it off this year but for next year I have arranged to have the members of the Hyde Park Robin Hoods, which won the semi-pro championship of Western Dutchess, given jobs by the press associations and some of the more famous papers. Even the Wall Street Journal has fallen for it and will assign Rube De Groff (formerly substitute catcher for the New York Yankees) to cover the President during that week end.

I am also making a special arrangement with Der Führer to drop no bombs on our diamond until after the sixth inning!

As ever yours,

Franklin D Roosevelt

Lowell Thomas, Esq.,
Rockefeller Center,
New York, New York.

The "Nine Old Men" won a memorable but "unimportant victory" over the "Prehistoric Sluggers" August 16, 1937, with acress Anna May Wong in the role of umpire.

Those attending the 1940 "Nine Old Men" game thought they were seeing F.D.R. (who often was on hand.) In this case it was impersonator Billy Van of vaudeville fame, with Gen. Theodore Roosevelt Jr. on the running board. Crowd and players were completely "taken in."

Besides a long-standing friendship, Lowell and Jack Dempsey share other mutual interests. Both worked at the Portland, richest of all Colorado gold mines. Both were taught boxing by fistic coach Morgan Williams.

Lowell also has been a close friend through the years with Dempsey's successor, Gene Tunney, star pitcher on his "Nine Old Men."

Lowell Thomas   Captain Eddie Rickenbacker   Sid Luckman   Bo McMillan

Coach, G. A.

In 1948 Sportsman-Tycoon G. A. "Dick" Richards, who then owned the Detroit Lions, put together his "dream team" of famous personalities. Front: Ernie McCoy, Ty Cobb. Frank Leahy and Father Cavanaugh of Notre Dame, Pres. John A. Hannah of Michigan State, Gov. Kim Sigler, George Halas of the Chicago Bears; Backs Lowell Thomas, Eddie Rickenbacker, Sid Luckman and Bo McMillan. "Coach" Richards on the right.

Long a football fan, here he is with Mrs. Thomas and Notre Dame president Father Hesburgh.

SECTION 9

The article which follows, you'll note, boasts one of the best "leads" in the book. Furthermore Al Hirshberg's profile got the full treatment—a cover in full color with Lowell selected as Argosy's "Giant of Adventure."

Anyway, the author with his beginning quickly captures attention and then keeps up his pace all through. It appeared in 1958.

Preceding it is a background sketch, with pictures, regarding a motion picture revolution—the "discovery" of Cinerama and the dawn of the wide screen era.

What Happened To Cinerama?

Interview by Norman Bowen

Norm: By the way, Lowell, whatever happened to Cinerama? As its "discoverer," producer, one-time President, and even referred to as its "father," would you mind telling us the "inside story"?

L. T.: You are right, Fred Wallwer was the creator of the stunning new process that revolutionized motion pictures. Fred gave birth to Cinerama, after which he went on experimenting with it for fourteen years. Then I came along, rediscovered Waller, whom I had known many years before, and helped get his exciting invention out of the laboratory. For years now, all over the world, Norm, I've been asked the question you have just put to me. It's impossible to give you an answer in a few words.

Norm: Obviously it was a sensation both in this country and abroad. What about all those record runs in New York, Detroit, Chicago, Los Angeles, London, Paris, Tokyo, Osaka and other cities, didn't it make money?

L. T.: It did make money all right, lots of it, that is, for the original group who controlled production and distribution. Then my early associates lost control. Those who took it over also did nothing but make money. However, aside from the equally thrilling stereophonic sound added by Hazard Reeves, not much research was done to improve it. Also there was confusion as to what to do with the fabulous new medium.

Norm: Didn't it bring on the so-called Wide Screen Era?

L. T.: Yes. In fact, as former President Hoover said when he saw our first one, THIS IS CINERAMA; "There have been four milestones: One—the discovery of motion pictures. Two—the addition of sound. Three—color. Four—Cinerama.

146

Norm: Then why has Cinerama disappeared?

L. T.:   The heads of the motion picture industry had decided, correctly I believe, that Cinerama was a special form of entertainment, not adaptable to the neighborhood theaters which were their basic market. Therefore, they passed it by. But, when my colleagues and I brought out the first Cinerama show it was such a sensational success that over night they decided they had made a mistake, changed their minds, and hurriedly began scouting for wide screen processes to save themselves from the ruin they thought they faced with TV.

However, my associates procrastinated and before they knew it had lost control. The new owners seemed to be even more confused. Then along came another owner who did a human thing. He put aside the magic Cinerama process, and simply exploited the name, which by then had become world famous.

Meanwhile, a fourth owner got control of the company. He also exploited the name, making money on Cinerama's fame as a result of our first pictures which had given audiences, for the first time, that new, extraordinary feeling of personal participation.

Since then—no Cinerama. However, a fifth group is now in control, and I am hoping they will realize what a gold mine this process was and still could be.

Some day, some day, some wise man again will take advantage of the magic of Cinerama.

As for the rest of that story, I will tell it in a year or two. More than forty years ago the elder Mr. Doubleday asked me to write an autobiography. This was after World War I and my experiences "with Lawrence in Arabia, with Allenby in Palestine," the German Revolution and then "The First World Flight." But, I laughed and said I was too young. Now I am sorry I didn't take him up on the offer, for I am sure I have forgotten a great deal that might have been fun to put in writing. At any rate, at long last I have agreed to attempt it, and the detailed story of Cinerama, how the brilliant Mike Todd was tossed out, and many other incidents, are likely to provide material for one or two chapters; a story hitherto untold.

Norm: I'd like to put in my order now for the first copy. I was overwhelmed by Cinerama and want to know the full story.

147

In the early Fifties he created a motion picture revolution with the introduction of Cinerama—wide screen with stereophonic sound. Here he presides at cake-cutting ceremony marking first year of the Broadway run of "This Is Cinerama." Left, Hazard Reeves, who developed the sound system; center, Fred Waller, inventor of the revolutionary Cinerama process that brought on the "wide screen era."

At opening of "The Seven Wonders of the World" with long-time Hollywood headliner Joan Crawford, now prominent in world of business.

Fifty Years of Adventure

By AL HIRSHBERG *Prominent American author and writer.*

The day will come when a compact man, with piercing blue eyes, wavy salt-and-pepper hair, a thin mustache and a voice like an organ, will stride briskly toward the pearly gates. The guardian angel will recognize him at once. "Here comes Lowell Thomas," he will say. "He's been everywhere else."

And the guardian angel won't be far wrong. Lowell Thomas is a fabulous, fascinating character who, at sixty-six, is celebrating the golden anniversary of his career of high adventure. Restless, nervous, possessor of vast stores of excess energy and a pair of the itchiest feet in the world, he will go anywhere, any time, under any conditions and by any transportation if there is a promise of finding something unusual at the other end.

To Thomas, everything is an adventure, including life itself. He wants to see everything there is to see in the world, do everything there is to do, learn everything there is to learn.

This is a multi-sided man with an overwhelming curiosity, a passion for adventure, an abiding interest in everything around him. He travels fast and far—he went around the world five times last year—because he's pressed for time. He has only one life to live, and he doesn't want to waste a single precious minute of it. He is incapable of standing still; he must go and go and go, stopping only to rest and store up enough energy to go and go and go some more.

America knows him best as a radio and television broadcaster, and well she might. Lowell Thomas, whose newscasts came every weekday from somewhere in the world, has been on the air in an unbroken line longer than anyone in the business. He began on September 29, 1930, when he succeeded the legendary Floyd Gibbons, radio's first daily newscaster, and he's been going ever since. His deep, resonant, "So long until tomorrow" is radio's most famous signoff. His voice has been heard by more people than any voice in the history of mankind. Seventy billion men, women and children have listened to him at one time or another during his twenty-eight years on the air and on the screen.

This alone would win Lowell everlasting fame, yet it forms only one segment of his complex life. Thomas is a platform personality and toastmaster who, if he cared to accept anywhere nearly all the invitations he receives, could devote the rest of his life to the platform and banquet table with profit. He is known from Broadway to Main Street as a movie producer and commentator, the man who was the voice of Fox Movietone News for years and whose travels have been immortalized through the immensely popular Cinerama series.

Among other things, he has been miner, editor, cook, janitor, reporter, athlete, cowboy, professor, soldier, flyer and explorer. He has written some fifty books. He has traveled by every known means of locomotion, from perambulator to pinto pony, from horseless carriage to helicopter, from rickshaw to roller coaster, from jitney to jet pursuit plane.

He has rubbed elbows with presidents and kings, with knights of the road and Knights of the Garter, with soldiers of fortune and sailors of misfortune. It is quite probable that he is on first-name terms with more people, famous and otherwise, than anyone alive, and he treats them all alike. Even though he is one of the world's most peripatetic personalities, his feet are set solidly on the ground, and his sense of values has never been warped. He is equally courteous to bellhops and bishops.

When he picks up his telephone in New York, where he maintains a Madison Avenue apartment, he always says, "Hello, how are you?", calling the operator by name, then gives his number. He has a similar greeting for the doorman, the janitor and anyone else who is around. He knows them all, and they know him.

This is the man who called Mr. Roosevelt "Franklin" before he was governor of New York, who made a journey with the Duke of Windsor when he was the Prince of Wales, and who personally delivered a message from the Dalai Lama of Tibet, one of his friends, to Harry S Truman, another.

Lowell Thomas collects friends with the eagerness of a philatelist collecting stamps. He would rather talk than eat, a most fortunate circumstance, for he makes the bulk of his living with his vocal chords. He uses them to make friends as well as money, and he now has plenty of both.

He lives the life the rest of us dream about, going where he pleases, when he pleases. Unlike most celebrities, who maintain strict, tight schedules and almost always know where they're going to be months in advance, Thomas maintains practically no schedule at all. His plans are so flexible that he can always change them on a few hours' notice.

He seldom puts himself into a spot he can't get out of in a hurry. He hates being tied down. He has to be free to move around, to accept spur-of-the moment invitations, to take a week-end trip to Timbuktu or go on a quick safari up the Congo or fly to the North Pole to fish through the ice, or go skiing in Chile or gold-digging in Honduras or diamond-mining in South Africa or skin-diving in Sumatra.

His favorite word is adventure, and pursuing it is his favorite occupation.

He got off to a pretty good start, for he was born next door to Annie Oakley, in Darke County, Ohio, on April 6, 1892. "I was only a baby when we moved out of there," he said, "so I can't say she had any great influence over me. But just the knowledge that I started out as a next-door neighbor to the world's most famous lady sharp-shooter seemed to mark me for something, I don't know what."

The mark became clearer when his parents took him to the gold fields of Colorado at an early age. Lowell's father, Dr. Harry G. Thomas, was a mining surgeon. The family home was at the time above Cripple Creek, which in those days was one of the wildest of all wildwest communities. There were scores of mines in the area, and each drew its quota of rough characters trying to hit the jackpot. The biggest business in town was done by saloons, gambling joints and whore houses, and few men wandered about without a weapon.

It was here, in the shadow of the great gold mines of the time— the Portland, the Anaconda, the Independence, the Cresson, the Golden Cycle and all the rest—that Lowell Thomas grew up and, in-deed, it was here that his appetite for adventure was whetted almost beyond reason. Everywhere he turned, he met exciting people, for there were no more colorful characters in the world than gold-miners of the era around the turn of the century. They floated from place to place, gathering stories as they moved, and, sooner or later, they found their way to Cripple Creek.

151

Even a youngster had to be careful. No matter where he came from, how good his background, how intelligent his parents or how fine his instincts, there were lessons he had to learn, not only for his own happiness, but for his very survival. Lowell Thomas could handle a gun before he was ten. He practically grew up on horseback. And he learned early never to wear his broadbrimmed hat squarely on his head.

"No matter what your age, you figured you had to *look* tough," he recalls. "I went by the saloons and the gambling joints and the houses of prostitution on my way to school every day, and you couldn't afford to let anyone think you were a sissy. So I've always worn my hat at that same jaunty angle."

Cripple Creek, of itself, would fire the imagination of a growing boy, but young Lowell had other incentives. He lived on a mountain side overlooking the Sangre de Cristo (Blood of Christ) Range, and every day of his life was spiced by a breathtaking view of mountains and sky.

"You could see for a hundred miles on a clear day," he said, "and I used to gaze at that changing panorama for hours and hours. All my life, snow-capped mountains have been as much a part of me as eating and sleeping and breathing. To this day, my heart pounds a little harder and my breath catches at the sight of mountains. I used to stand outside my house and stare, and wonder what was on the other side of the range. I've been wanting to see the other side ever since."

As he grew older, he grew more curious, not only about the world immediately around him, but about everything else. From his parents, both of whom were once country schoolteachers, he inherited a thirst for knowledge which has never left him. His father was his idol, a man interested in everything to the day of his death. At eighty-three, Dr. Thomas was still studying—special work at Oxford and other universities abroad.

He unwittingly gave his son one key to success when he taught him to speak with resonance and clarity. "There's nothing more grating on the ear than a poor speaking voice," he used to say. "Your voice is the sounding board of your personality. Make it something to be proud of."

Lowell took him at his word, and his voice became his fortune. He was a restless youth, anxious to get started, without really knowing where he was going. When he was eleven, he got a job on the Victor *Record.* In later years, he became editor of the paper. At one period the editor of a rival daily was Ralph Carr, who eventually became one of Colorado's outstanding governors.

Thomas first went to work in the mines when he was thirteen, and it was then that he really got to know the men who spent their lives seeking gold. They told him tales of life in other parts of the world, particularly Honduras and the Klondike and the Transvaal, the big gold-producing centers of the time outside the continental limits of the United States. Long before he first visited the Klondike, he felt he knew the place.

With men like Tex Rickard, Abe Attell, Eddie Eagan and others moving in and out of Cripple Creek, Thomas developed an early interest in boxing. To this day, he doesn't miss a big fight if he can help it. When MacArthur came home from the Pacific, he went to a fight with L. T. In Colorado, Thomas took boxing lessons from a man named Morgan Williams. Years later, when he became friendly with Jack Dempsey, he discovered that Williams had also been a Dempsey ring instructor.

Thomas loves all sports, but especially those in which he can participate himself. He took up skiing in his forties, and has been a keen enthusiast ever since. He is on the board of three or more ski developments in Vermont, one in Canada and one in the Sierras and he never lets a year go by without spending time at ski centers somewhere. He has worked with ski troops both here and in Europe. More than once, he has suffered injury on the slopes, including broken legs and twice a broken shoulder, but these have not dampened his ardor.

"Once a ski fan, always a ski fan," he says. "When the sport gets you, it gets you forever."

Flying fascinated him. Long before the rest of the world became aware of air travel, he was bouncing around in open cockpits, often with pioneering daredevils who saw in the air the railroad tracks of the future. He got to know practically all the early American airmen and wrote their stories. These friendships later stood him in good stead, for many of the men he knew as daredevils later became the highest ranking officers in the United States Army Air Force.

At fifteen, after working for a time in the Empire State gold mine, near Pike's Peak, he left home for the first time to go to college. He worked his way through the University of Northern Indiana at Valparaiso, paying his tuition by toiling as a janitor, salesman and short-order cook in a railroad restaurant. Two years later, he had both a bachelor's and a master's degree. With these, he returned to Cripple Creek.

"The degrees were very helpful," he says. "They qualified me to operate a pick and shovel. I went back to the mines because I wanted to learn more from those wonderful guys who wandered in, dug, and told stories for a while, then wandered out."

One day, the publisher of the Victor *Record* asked him, "How much are you making in the mines?"

"Three dollars a day. Ninety a month."

"I'll give you ninety-five to come and work for me."

So Thomas went back to the newspaper business, and, ever since, has been a newsman. He later moved over to the *News*, the opposition paper, where he became editor before leaving Cripple Creek. He left the paper to go back to college for two more arts degrees, then the law, and taught for a while in a Chicago law school. Then, after two expeditions to Alaska, he went to Princeton to study constitutional law. He taught there, too, while he tried to decide what to do next.

"I took constitutional law because I intended to enter public life," he said. "But while I was at Princeton, I realized the law wasn't for me. It was too confining.

"I'd have to sit behind a desk. I had to be free to move around. That was when I decided to stay in the newspaper world."

But he still thought he needed more formal education. One graduate course at the University of Denver turned out to be one of the most important moves of his life. While he was there, he met a co-ed named Frances Ryan, then a freshman. He married her in 1917.

He went overseas as a correspondent during the first World War. There, he looked for trouble, and had no problem finding it. Late in 1917, in Venice, which was deserted because the Austrians were only a few miles away, he happened to see a bulletin pinned to a sandbag in front of the Cathedral of San Marco. It told how the British had sent a new commander-in-chief, General Edmund H. H. Allenby, to take over in Egypt.

Thomas had never been in Egypt, nor, for that matter, in any

154

of the Near East countries. He had heard of Allenby as a brilliantly successful cavalry commander, first in the Boer War and later on the western front, and he knew there would be excitement and adventure in store for anyone who followed this British leader. Thomas got himself attached to Allenby's army and, within a week, was on his way across the Mediterranean aboard a British man-o'-war.

He got excitement and adventure until it was coming out of his ears. Allenby's men were a polyglot collection of warriors from almost every corner of the British Empire. Thomas watched them using their then modern equipment fo fight the Turks in ancient lands familiar to him up to that time only through his study of the Bible. He saw action with Anzac cavalrymen, the Bikanir camel corps and plain cockneys on horseback, battling in places like Bethlehem and Jericho, the Mount of Olives and the Holy City.

Thomas was the first American—indeed, one of the first mortals —ever to fly over the Sinai Desert. He became one of the historians of the Palestinian campaign, and, as such, was the first writer to tell of one of the most obscure, yet interesting phases of World War I.

One day, as he was walking along Christian Street in Jerusalem, a group of Arab sheiks approached him. At first, they all looked alike, then suddenly, Thomas noticed a young, beardless Bedouin wearing the curved sword of a Prince of Mecca. A closer look disclosed a pair of blue eyes.

This was no ordinary sheik, and Thomas was no man to let him go by without trying to find out more about him.

And that's how Lowell Thomas became the first westerner to meet the fabulous Lawrence of Arabia in his adopted surroundings.

Soon after, Thomas left Allenby and joined Lawrence, then absolutely unknown to the world. This young Oxford archaeologist who became a sheik of the desert and a fiery, inspiring Bedouin leader, might be unknown to this day if it weren't for Lowell Thomas. For he was the first to bring the saga of T. E. Lawrence out of the desert. He told it all over the world in an illustrated production before packed audiences. Night after night, he filled first Covent Garden Opera House and later the huge Albert Hall in London, where he had been invited after a British impressario heard him tell the story in New York. After a long London run, he visited Scotland, Ireland and Wales, then, with his wife, made a tour of the Empire telling the Lawrence-Allenby tale in Australia, India, Burma,

Malaya, and on around the globe.

It was the Lawrence-Allenby story which first made Lowell Thomas truly world-famous. Through it, he met kings and maharajahs, generals and admirals, presidents and prime ministers. His book, "Lawrence of Arabia," became an instant hit and still lives as something of a classic.

Now Thomas no longer had to seek adventure; it sought him. He was invited everywhere, given carte blanche to move where he pleased and do as he pleased. He chose to go to Germany. The war was over, but the Reich was still under Allied blockade in the North Sea. Thomas ran the blockade, got to Kiel, and followed the German revolution all the way to the mountains of Bavaria. At Nuremburg he met another fabulous character to introduce to the rest of the world. It was Lowell Thomas who made Count Luckner famous. His book about the most colorful raider of the first World War, "Count Luckner, the Sea Devil," was another best seller.

His Lawrence-Allenby tour, in the twenties was his first trip around the world. He and his wife—who went everywhere with him until 1923, when Lowell, Jr. was born in London—made a hundred sea voyages together, then stopped counting. Later she continued to travel with him whenever it was possible. Lowell, Jr. often went along, and the thirty-five-year-old son of a famous father is now an explorer and adventurer of no small prominence in his own right, veteran of a dozen expeditions.

Since high-speed travel became common-place, Thomas has lost track of his trips around the world. In 1924 he became historian for the American flyers who won the international race to be the first to go around the world by air. Thomas' book about the trip was to go around the world by air. Thomas' book about the trip was another success.

His next world tour was a typical example of his flexibility of movement, to say nothing of his remarkable connections and magnetic flair for adventure. After the Normandy invasion of 1944, Thomas, dead-tired, ran into his old friend, General Jimmy Doolittle, in France.

"I'm going 'around the world," Doolittle said casually, "How about coming along?"

"I'm bushed," Thomas said. "I've got to go home and rest up."

"That's all right," the general said. "I'm not leaving right away."

"Wire me when you do," Thomas said, "and I'll let you know."

Two days after his arrival in the States, Thomas got a wire to meet Doolittle in Casablanca. He forgot his fatigue and left at once. On the way, he met General Benjamin Giles of the U. S. Army Air Force, who bet him a case of champagne he wouldn't catch up with Doolittle until he general got to Washington.

"I lost the bet," says Thomas, "but I had a whale of a time."

Doolittle was ordered to push on before Thomas arrived in North Africa. Here began a chase that Thomas couldn't hope to win. He had red tape to unravel and radio broadcasts to transcribe, while Doolittle just kept on going. In Calcutta, Thomas read that Doolittle was in Washington.

He ran into a cavalry colonel he knew who invited him on a trip to the China-Tibet frontier. After this detour, Thomas spent some time at Generalissimo Chiang Kai-shek's headquarters in Chungking, crossed China by jeep and stayed for a while, then flew to Manila by night. The plane he rode in was the first to fly out over the Japanese army. From Manila, Thomas went to Guam, where his plane landed beside one marked *Argonaut IV*.

"Here my transportation problems were over," Thomas said. "The *Argonaut IV* was Hap Arnold's plane. He was an old flying pal of mine. He had flown me long ago, when he was a young officer under Billy Mitchell."

He made the last leg of the trip with General Arnold. The whole junket had taken Doolittle a matter of days. It took Thomas three months.

No man can live as Lowell Thomas lives without taking his life in his hands. And no one knows better than Thomas the danger that lurks in each new expedition. Thomas has often been injured in accidents of one sort or another, once in a plane crash on the Spanish desert, and he takes these injuries in stride.

But once it seemed certain that death was around the corner. If it had not been for his son, he probably never would have lived to tell the story.

In 1949, Lowell and Lowell, Jr. were invited to the forbidden city of Lhasa, the original Shangri-La, in the mysterious country of Tibet. It was a journey Thomas had been wanting to make all his life.

Nothing unusual—for Lowell Thomas, at least—happened on the

trip to Tibet. His party made it on schedule, and he and his son were royally entertained after they got there. Just before they left for the return trip, Tsarong Shapé, who had once held the office corresponding to prime minister of Tibet, asked if there was anything they needed.

"Just one thing," said Thomas through his interpreter. "We're fed up with the horses we used coming in. They were trail-bound, walking nose-to-tail, and that's not much fun. I notice you use tall mules. My son and I would like to buy two, and ride them out. We'll sell them in India."

"I won't sell you any mules," Tsarong said, "because you will get cheated when you try to sell them in India. But I'll lend you two, and send someone along to bring them back."

While he was about it, the former Tibetan official sent a couple of half-trained native horses along for his man to sell at Yatung, near the border. The party started out, with Thomas on one of the borrowed mules. Within two days, he was bored.

"All mules are alike," he said. "Even tall, handsome ones. These mules were trail-bound forty-eight hours after we left."

He turned to the guide, and said, "How about my riding one of those horses you're taking to sell for Tsarong."

"All right. But I must warn you," the Tibetan replied. "They're not broken."

"I've ridden unbroken horses before," Thomas said, "so maybe that won't matter."

"Go ahead," said his companion. "Maybe you'll be all right, but it takes five men to hold this horse while you mount him. But once you're aboard, he is all right."

Two days later, Thomas absent-mindedly started to mount the horse alone on a 17,000-foot pass. The animal wheeled and tossed him over the edge of the trail, smashing his hip. Much later, in India, they found it was broken in eight places.

"My son Lowell, saved my life," he said. "He held me in his arms most of that night to keep me from getting pneumonia in the cold, then took complete charge of the expedition, which he converted into a rescue party. Also, he made a litter, and on some air mattresses, they carried me across the Tibetan plateau and over the Himalayas. We were twenty days getting to Calcutta, and from there we flew on to New York, where I was operated on. I'm lucky to be alive after that one."

For years, Thomas has had the largest listening audience of anyone in radio. The most amazing tribute to its size came one night in the thirties, when he was doing a broadcast with a telegraphic background from the Western Union building in downtown Manhattan. Before the show ended, it was announced that anyone who wanted to send a personal message to Lowell Thomas by wire was welcome to do so. It would all be on the company.

In a matter of minutes, the wires became so clogged that extra help had to be put on to handle the sudden surge of traffic. More than 262,000 telegrams poured in during the next few hours. If they had been paid for, they would have cost $500,000.

Thomas had the messages sent to his place at Quaker Hill, but he never got to read them. The house where he stored them burned down a year or so later, and the telegrams were lost in the fire.

Today, Thomas lives near Pawling, New York, in a home landscaped by his own golf course. His next-door neighbor is Thomas E. Dewey, former governor of New York and twice Republican candidate for President. The two are close friends and frequent golf partners.

Politics makes strange bedfellows, but association with Lowell Thomas makes stranger. Sworn enemies sometimes meet—and are even civil to each other—at Thomas' place. For several years, he and Franklin D. Roosevelt, whose Hyde Park home was not far away, managed rival teams in an annual softball game which attracted world-wide attention.

"I'll give you thirty cents for your first baseman," F.D.R. said to Thomas one day. "That's all he's worth."

Even the first baseman laughed when he heard about it. He was Hamilton Fish. Roosevelt was so anxious to get him out of Congress that soon after that he redistricted Fish's constituency so that he would be defeated.

"I like to bring people together," Thomas said, smiling. "All sorts of funny things happen. But that's another story."

"But that's another story." This, like his famous "So long until tomorrow," is one of Lowell Thomas' trade marks.

He will have another story to tell as long as he lives—and maybe longer. Perhaps some day, this man, more fascinating than the places he's been to, more interesting than the people he's met, more fluent in the one language he speaks than any multilinguist, will be telling stories to the guardian angel.

And when he arrives at the pearly gates, even then I suspect that he'll be packing them in.

Heading for the barn, with Governor Dewey when he was Presidential candidate and only missed victory by a few votes.

With Helen Hayes, "the First Lady of the American Theatre," whose author-husband, Charles MacArthur, was a Chicago newspaper reporter along with Lowell, Floyd Gibbons and others just before World War I.

He has had the distinction of enjoying a single sponsor for longer periods than anyone in radio or TV history—Sun Oil Company, Joseph Pew Jr., president for 15 years and General Motors for 17 years. Here the Marquis degli d'Albizzi, Mr. and Mrs. Pew and Lowell.

Receiving another, this one from distinguished jurist Charles E. Murphy.

One of the greatest swimmers of all time, "Duke" Kahanamoku, on outrigger at Waikiki.

Gonzalez Studio

The "Sea Devil" of World War I, the subject of another Lowell Thomas best seller, published in 1927. Count von Luckner, with Lowell Jr. and Sr.

Honors have come from many foreign countries. Here the French Consul, General Charles de Fontnouvell, in traditional fashion, makes him a Knight of the Legion of Honor, May 5, 1938.

He discusses the latest space conquest with General Douglas MacArthur, shortly before the latter's death.

Everest Conqueror Sir Edmund Hillary, rocket expert Werner Von Braun, Antarctic explorer, Capt. Finn Ronne, and New Guinea expert Tom Gilliard, chat with Lowell Thomas after Explorers banquet.

SECTION 10

Crammed into studios, attics, workrooms and assorted corners of Lowell's spacious home and various offices are clippings and pictures from the press of the world.

Loweel has been providing more copy for other journalists down through the decades than he has turned out himself. Which is considerable.

Included as a mere sample of foreign press coverage, which the American public seldom sees, is the following from the Bombay, India MIRROR, in 1965.

Lowell Thomas: All Round Genius

By G. SRINIVAS RAO *India writer and author.*

"We live on an exciting and fantastic planet," declares Mr. Lowell Thomas in his recent message to this writer, "every part of which has something special about it. But, of all the countries in the world, I still feel as I did when I first went there nearly half-a-century ago, that India—the Hindustan peninsula—from Cape Comorin to the crest of the Himalayas, from the Chin Hills to the Khyber and Hunza, is the most thrilling and dramatic part of the globe. This is true mainly because it is a region of such startling contrast. Each time I visit Southern Asia, which I sometimes do two or three times in one year, I make the journey with as much curiosity as though I had never been there before."

These dynamic words give a clue to the remarkable personality who has often been hailed as a "Living Legend." Very few people anywhere in the world at anytime, could achieve such a fabulous name as Lowell Thomas. One still wonders if such a soul does really breathe on this planet. Fortunately, this great man is still very active and continues to inspire us with his many-sided roles.

Going around the world in search of adventure and fun, producing scores of books with amazing facility and speed, exploring new regions to uncover hidden secrets, photographing and reporting on the customs and festivals of cannibals in the remotest zones, broadcasting and fact-finding, are some of the main features of his wonderful life. Love of adventure and the courage to face anything are a part of his blood.

The life-story of Lowell Thomas reads like a fairy tale. While the legends have associated the place of his birth to the Arabian Desert itself, he was in fact born in Ohio, U.S.A. on April 6, 1892. Soon after the birth of Lowell, his father, Harry Thomas, graduated in medicine and moved to Cripple Creek in Colorado to set up practice. The young boy grew up here, meeting strange people almost everyday, carrying a gun and reading all kinds of books bought and given by his thoughtful father. All these helped the boy to develop his skills and speak with vigour in the years to come.

Returning to Ohio with his mother at fifteen, Mr. Thomas attended a variety of schools and bagged degrees and honours from the universities of North Indiana, Denver and Princeton in the quickest possible time. He also studied Law at Chicago and simultaneously took up the job of reporting for a local journal. True to the American character, he always earned while he learned and specialized in the art of effective speaking, which today helps him to mystify the audience with his broadcasts.

With the First World War not far from sight, at which Lowell Thomas showed amazing skill of penetrating through the toughest zones and reporting accurately, his study of constitutional law came to a close. He became an instructor of public-speaking and left for Alaska to embark on his new hobby of making movies. He also courted with a religious zeal and won the love of Fran Ryan, his friend at Denver College. Soon they got married and left for Europe, at the request of the American Government, to report on War.

The Great War opened new vistas of exploration and adventure for Lowell Thomas. He saw and did wonderful things and met, among others, an outstanding personality who has now become famous as the Lawrence of Arabia.

The two daring personalities met for the first time in Jerusalem. Mr. Thomas was struck with the slender but arresting figure whom he later knew as T. E. Lawrence, the British scholar, soldier and diplomat of immense worth. Soon they became good friends, and, while Lawrence fought in the desert on the side of Feisal, the Arab Chief, Lowell Thomas joined him in the successful campaign and covered the events in words and by film.

The very daring but remarkably shy Lawrence would probably have lived and died in obscurity, had not Mr. Thomas *discovered* him and brought his story to the limelight. The book of Lowell Thomas entitled *With Lawrence in Arabia* has become a classic and has already run into more than a hundred editions. Similarly, the film has brought the "discovered" and the "discoverer" endless fortune.

Mr. Thomas is like a machine that knows no fatigue. Author of more than forty books and countless magazine-articles, today, his name in the realm of literature is permanent, while his regular, colorful radio-talks, are refreshingly memorable. To collect material for his talks and shows, Lowell Thomas has covered virtually every nook and corner of the world. In 1957, and again in 1963, he undertook the most awful expedition to New Guinea where he lived in the company of the cannibal *friends* who had earlier eaten members of a rival tribe at a dinner party. In moving words and pictures he has captured their ghastly way of life, their feasts and their fanfare.

Since then, Lowell Thomas has gone to the North Pole, to the heights of the Himalayas, to the Mountains of the Moon in Africa, and even to the forbidden land of Tibet, where his friend was none other than the Dalai Lama. It appears, that there is hardly any place now left which has not receive his soft footfalls!!

Today, having completed seventy-three long years of action and authority, Lowell Thomas is busy as ever. Much of his time is spent in reading and reporting, swimming, skiing, dancing, meeting old friends and helping them solve their problems—all of which are a passion with him. A many-sided geniuṣ as he is, Mr. Thomas is sought by the high and low for counsel and wisdom. His deeds have become legends which seem to grow, as time advances.

O. SOGLOW

Prosper Buranelli, for 30 years a close associate. By Artist McClelland Barclay.

*"Perhaps the most brilliant, the most fabulous human being I
ever knew was my colleague Prosper Buranelli," says Lowell.*

*Prosper, who was with Lowell as colleague and companion for
more than 30 years, died in 1961 after a Quaker Hill evening
with Governor Dewey, Norman Vincent Peale, Edward R. Murrow
and Lowell. Wherever Prosper Buranelli was there was laughter
and sparkling conversations.*

*"He was a genius—with an encyclopedic mind. His knowledge
of music, literature, art, philosophy, history, mathematics, and many
other subjects even including women, was almost unique. Along
with all this he had humility and charm; I never knew his equal,"
Lowell added.*

*Among his many accomplishments was the launching of the
crossword puzzle craze in America, propelled by way of* The New
York World *and the publishing firm of Simon and Schuster. It was
one of the top successes of the Post-World War I period.*

169

Temporarily tired of traveling and out looking for their first home, they passed Clover Brook farm in 1926 and decided this was it.

These rolling hills of "The Lower Berkshires" in Dutchess County, New York, have been home to Lowell and Fran more than 40 years. Looking down on the domain he took over from the estate of Skyscraper Builder Fred F. French.

Canoeing and relaxing on his private lake. As usual, the news goes along . . .

In the Malay Forest in the early Twenties, Fran and a Sakai maiden, member of a Pygmy tribe.

Knutson

He returned to the Rockies in the late Forties to officiate at a ground-breaking for a big new ore reduction mill. Mrs. Thomas (next to mike) watches. At left, Ralph Carr, one-time rival editor in Victor and, at this time, one of Colorado's ablest governors.

Here's L.T. and Fran at a luncheon in their honor back in the Thirties in Victor, Colorado, standing behind Governor Ralph Carr, and Editor Harry Denny on the right. Fred Mazulla snapped the picture.

Fred & Jo. Mazzul

With portrait of the fabled markswoman, Annie Oakley, who was "born next door" to his birthplace in Greenville, Ohio.

The Cincinnati Times-Star Saturday July 31, 1943

Many names of prominent Republicans are being suggested as winning material for the GOP convention. While most of them are good and would make satisfactory executives, yet they lack a nation-wide popularity.

Now I want to suggest the name of an outstanding American, one who is known in every state, city, town and hamlet and even in the remote farm an mining districts of continental United States and in all of our outlying possessions, thus making it unnecessary to build up a following.

As a postwar administrator of the affairs of this country, he is eminently fitted because of his firsthand knowledge of conditions in the warring countries. A man who knows and is known by all of the great and near-great in about all of the countries of the world. A man with a pleasing voice and a captivating personality. A native Buckeye and for a short time a resident Hoosier. A simon-pure Republican and a New Deal foe. I nominate Lowell Thomas. How about it, boys and girls of the GOP?

173

Greenville, Ohio, asked him to return home in the early Thirties to accept honors as a home-town boy who made good. He had only one request—that he have a chance to play another game of pool with Jelly Burns—a legendary ·local who, in the old Three-I league had pitched and won baseball's longest game (22 innings) and who always managed to beat him at pool. Lowell had the first shot, "scratched" the cue-ball in the side-pocket, whereupon Jelly cleared the table. In front enjoying the debacle are Fred Coppock, Greenville's number one benefactor, and Frances Thomas.

With Colorado Governor Ralph Carr. Once rival editors in gold mining town of Victor, Colo., the pair maintained close friendship ever after.

Fred M. Mazzulla

With Thomas J. Watson, founder of IBM and a long-time friend.

Greeting Lowell on his return to Ohio was Ex-Governor James Cox, who ran for President of the United States in 1928, and a group of Dayton businessmen.

Here Lowell's sister, Pherbia, a world traveler in her own right, addresses distinguished audience at a New York World's Fair banquet. Beside her Ambassador Wm. D. Pawley, Mrs. William Brown Meloney, founder *This Week Magazine;* and her brother. She is now married to industrialist Raymond Thornburg and also lives on Quaker Hill.

With General and Mrs. Theodore Roosevelt Jr. The son of Teddy Roosevelt led the famous First Division ashore at Normandy on D-Day and died shortly afterward.

Gonzalez Studio

Lowell Jr., his mother, his wife Tay Pryor and Lowell Sr., in study of home. Lamp stand is the ivory "tooth" of a narwhal, rifled like gun barrel. Shade pictures include Antarctic mountains named for Lowell, also island in the Arctic.

Akin Hall, non-denominational Church remodeled and moved by Lowell and Fran to present site overlooking Harlem Valley and Catskill Mountains to the west. Huge Victorian Inn once occupied same spot.

With Semon E. Knudsen, executive vice president of General Motors and a son of former president William Knudsen.

Harlow Curtice, former chairman of the board of General Motors, L.T. and Charles S. Mott, director and largest single stockholder.

Holding award presented to David Sarnoff of R.C.A.; at right, Frederick R. Kappel, former chairman of the board of A.T.&T.

L.T. launching first passenger flight around the world. Directly behind him are Juan Trippe, publishers Frank Gannett, Gardner Cowles and Roy Howard. On the left is Edwin D. Canham, editor of the *Christian Science Monitor;* behind him is Maurice T. Moore, chairman of the board of Time, Inc.; and at the top Barry Faris of INS. Electra, Lowell's secretary, is on steps and to her right, James Stahlman, *Nashville Banner* publisher.

Newly-elected governor of Illinois Adlai Stevenson, second from left, shared speaking honors with L.T., second from right, at Chicago Press Veterans 10th Annual Dinner at LaSalle Hotel, Dec. 4, 1948. Sitting beside L.T. is his one-time City Editor, the famous Richard J. Finnegan. John Delaney of *Chicago Daily News* presiding.

Recipient of more than 20 honorary degrees. He is here honored by Boston University, along with Thomas J. Watson, founder of IBM and Juan Trippe, founder of Pan American Airways.

John Stuart Cloud

(Lowell Thomas, dean of American radio broadcasters, and America's leading adventurer, is praised in the editorial which appears below. The editorial is by Albro Greggory, of the Juneau Empire. Lowell Thomas is no stranger to the Yukon having gone down the river in 1912. He is also a member of the White-horse Ski Club, and ran the rapids in the years before the dam was built.)

One of America's greatest adventurers, writers and commentators is Lowell Thomas, pioneer of radio broadcasting and a regular Alaska visitor.

If asked, I would say that Lowell Thomas is the most interesting man I know. And I am sure that most people who know him would agree.

How old is he? In years I could say, but I prefer the term "ageless," for that is what Lowell Thomas is.

Now Lowell comes to the fore once again, in the upcoming Argosy magazine. He has written what turns out to be an obituary although he did not plan it that way.

His subject is this nationally circulated magazine is none other than the strong-hearted Leonhard Seppala, the greatest sled dog racer in the world. Seppala died in Seattle Saturday.

We don't usually build up stories appearing in magazines. But there are two reasons for urging one and all to buy Argosy. They are (1) the fact that Lowell Thomas is the author, and (2) the subject, Seppala, the stouthearted little man from Nome who first came to public attention when he made the race for the Norton Sound town with serum to combat an epidemic of diphtheria.

Thomas puts the record straight. For many years, said Argosy editors, the wrong driver got the credit for the Nome serum dash. Thomas convinced them that it was, indeed, the great Seppala who was the Hero of Nome.

So Thomas has done this, the greatest story of a great little guy who really made North Country history before he put away the harness and breathed his last.

All of Alaska is proud of Sepp and proud of his accomplishments. We'd guess that Thomas was the little man's greatest friend. His story is a masterpiece, all of which you would expect from Lowell Thomas, "The Most Interesting Man I Know."

—A.B.G.

Bill Mark

Another globe-trotting friend: His Eminence Cardinal Spellman, the Marco Polo of the Catholic Church and Monseignor Ahearn.

On June 15, 1965, Capital Cities Broadcasting Corporation "went on the Big Board," the New York Stock Exchange. Attending the ceremony were, left Keith Funston, Exchange President; L.T. co-founder and Director of CCB, and his long time colleague Frank M. Smith, a co-founder and company chairman. "Cap Cities" includes some of the most successful and important television and radio stations in America.

Lowell Jr., an Alaskan state senator, addressing GOP National Convention in San Francisco, 1964.

This picture ties in with the three Presidential letters in the beginning of the book. With Eddie Rickenbacker, Arthur Godfrey and Gov. Nelson Rockefeller, the night of the Waldorf dinner in his honor.

Bill Mark

Both lead busy lives as writers and broadcasters, but Lowell Sr. and Jr. arrange to get together whenever they can schedule a crossing of paths. The above taken in the Spring of 1949, shortly before they made their expedition across the Himalayas to Lhasa, then the Dalai Lama's Shangri-La.

THE ALASKAN LOWELL *by Norm Bowen*

It was the first week in May, and the elder Lowell had been at Alta, Utah, his favorite ski area. As he does every year, he had been looking for Spring snow and long sunny days. But all over the West, the weather-man fooled us this year. At higher altitudes it still seemed like mid-winter, with deep powder snow, and avalanches, one of which L.T. and his party had escaped by a matter of moments. Now we were at the Salt Lake airport, and after checking his skis and gear, we were talking about his son, who had interrupted a coast-to-coast speaking tour to ski with him at Alta, and his wife who would be waiting for him at New York. He remarked how the two of them had had far more influence over his life during the past five decades than anyone else. This being the case, I thought why not include a profile of each.

A week later, I flew to New York, and after talking this over with Fran Thomas, I concluded it would take a full book to do anything like justice to the subject. Her adventures have been almost as numerous as his; she has been nearly everywhere in the world, has come in contact with hundreds, perhaps thousands, of interesting and unusual people. Moreover, she is a natural born story-teller, with a lively sense of humor. So, another book there should be.

As for the Alaskan Lowell, I met him only for a moment, at the Hotel Utah, just after he had come down from our spectacular mountains around Alta. All I know about him has been gained from reading material turned over to me by Electra, who presides over

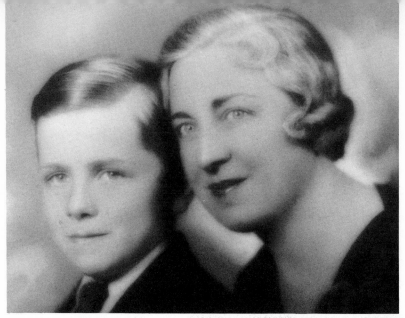

The two who have had the greatest influence on his life during the past five decades, his wife and their son.

the studio on Quaker Hill. From this I quickly discovered that a biography also should be written—or better still an autobiography—before L.T.-the Younger-is any older.

One thing seemed to stand out in all that I read—how he has shown leadership qualities since early childhood, first as a perennial class president all through his grade school years; at the same time colonel of one of the best known junior military organizations in America, to which such notables have belonged as the Rockefeller brothers, Ambassador Averell Harriman, the present head of the Metropolitan Museum, and hundreds of others. In fact, I read he was the youngest colonel in the history of The Knickerbocker Greys.

During the war he trained DeGaulle's Free French airmen, and in the years since the war has had a unique panorama of experience as a member, and often head, of some 20 expeditions—North Pole, South Pole, and to most of the remote parts of the globe. At age twenty-six he was offered a college presidency. Today, in his early 40s, he is a leader of life in our largest state, where he and his family make their home.

His father remarked to me how nothing made his hair stand on end quite so quickly as to hear someone say: "Oh, aren't you glad you son is following in your footsteps?" Said Lowell-the-Elder, "in aviation, in mountaineering, and in public service, he has gone so far ahead of me it isn't even funny."

So, I'm limiting my comments on the two people who meant so much to him to the suggestion that each deserves a separate book.

LOWELL THOMAS' LIST OF BOOKS

1. WITH LAWRENCE IN ARABIA   1924
2. THE FIRST WORLD FLIGHT   1924/25
3. BEYOND KHYBER PASS   1925
4. COUNT LUCKNER, THE SEA DEVIL   1927
5. EUROPEAN SKYWAYS   1927
6. THE BOY'S LIFE OF COLONEL LAWRENCE   1927
7. ADVENTURES IN AFGHANISTAN FOR BOYS   1928
8. RAIDERS OF THE DEEP   1928
9. THE SEA DEVIL'S FO'C'S'LE   1929
10. WOODFILL OF THE REGULARS   1929
11. THE HERO OF VINCENNES   1929
12. THE WRECK OF THE DUMARU   1930
13. LAUTERBACH OF THE CHINA SEA   1930
14. INDIA—LAND OF THE BLACK PAGODA   1930
15. ROLLING STONE   1931
16. TALL STORIES   1931
17. KABLUK OF THE ESKIMO   1932
18. THIS SIDE OF HELL   1932
19. OLD GIMLET EYE: THE ADVENTURES OF
      GENERAL SMEDLEY BUTLER   1933
20. BORN TO RAISE HELL   1933
21. THE UNTOLD STORY OF EXPLORATION   1935
22. FAN MAIL   1935
23. A TRIP TO NEW YORK WITH BOBBY AND BETTY   1936
24. MEN OF DANGER   1936
25. KIPLING STORIES AND A LIFE OF KIPLING   1936
26. SEEING CANADA WITH LOWELL THOMAS   1936
27. SEEING INDIA WITH LOWELL THOMAS   1936
28. SEEING JAPAN WITH LOWELL THOMAS   1937
29. SEEING MEXICO WITH LOWELL THOMAS   1937
30. ADVENTURES AMONG THE IMMORTALS   1937
31. HUNGRY WATERS   1937
32. WINGS OVER ASIA   1937
33. MAGIC DIALS   1939
34. IN NEW BRUNSWICK WE'LL FIND IT   1939
35. SOFT BALL! SO WHAT?   1940
36. HOW TO KEEP MENTALLY FIT   1940
37. STAND FAST FOR FREEDOM   1940
38. PAGEANT OF ADVENTURE   1940
39. PAGEANT OF LIFE   1941
40. PAGEANT OF ROMANCE   1943
41. THESE MEN SHALL NEVER DIE   1943
42. BACK TO MANDALEY   1951
43. GREAT TRUE ADVENTURES   1955
44. THE STORY OF THE NEW YORK THRUWAY   1955
45. SEVEN WONDERS OF THE WORLD   1956
46. HISTORY AS YOU HEARD IT   1957
47. THE STORY OF THE ST. LAWRENCE SEAWAY   1957
48. THE VITAL SPARK   1959
49. SIR HUBERT WIKINS, A BIOGRAPHY   1961
50. MORE GREAT TRUE ADVENTURES   1963
51. BOOK OF THE HIGH MOUNTAINS   1964

Epilogue

Lowell Thomas was waiting at the Salt Lake Airport for his plane which would take him back to New York and his busy schedule of broadcasts, books, banquets, films, speaking engagements and expeditions. For several weeks he had been skiing at Alta in between his daily news broadcasts.

Earlier we had been talking about Lowell's unusual father, who drilled him, while still a lad in Colorado's gold mining district of Cripple Creek, in public speaking and the arts and sciences, kindling the intense interest Lowell has since had in the world around him and its people.

"This is a story I have never told about my father," he confided.

"After I had made my first real money in London with my Lawrence-Allenby presentation (at the age of 28), I had an idea.

"I got in touch with the American University in Beirut, Lebanon and told them I wanted to endow a lecture chair in medicine. The only conditions I imposed were three:

"1) That it be known as the Allenby Chair (after the Allied liberator of the Holy Land in World War I whose historic 'Last Crusade' I covered).

"2) That the donor should remain anonymous, and

"3) That the first recipient should be Dr. Harry George Thomas of Victor, Colorado.

"The University quickly agreed and father was soon notified. He went to Beirut and had several wonderful years in the Near East.

"I never told him what I had done. And I don't know if he ever guessed.

"But recently I was in Lebanon again. I thought I would drop by the University and talk to anyone who might remember my father. No one did. They had all passed on.

"However, they looked up the records—and there it was: the Allenby Chair of Medicine, endowed by an anonymous *Englishman!* Why an Englishman? Because I had sent the funds from London, I suppose.

"But of course you can't use that story."

We couldn't but we did.

It illustrates a life-long trait of Lowell's and it is essential to your knowing him.

187